THE
Pet-Friendly
Garden

FOREWORD BY JOHN NOAKES

To pet-lovers and gardeners everywhere!

What a great idea this book is! I'm surprised no-one has thought of this before. The chances are that, like me, if you love pets you like gardening, and vice versa. So it makes a lot of sense to know how to make your garden a pleasure for your pets to be in as well as a pleasure for you to spend time in.

That's why I love this book so much. I've always made a lot of room in my life for my pets – in fact, pets and gardens go together like fish and chips, and life is very different without them. I now feel it is better to remember past times fondly and keep the garden as though Shep were still here with me.

This book is full of good, common-sense advice on how to prepare a garden to be a proper environment for all sorts of pets, from how to plan its structure to what plants and flowers to put in.

So get out there and get gardening – and may you all, owners and pets, enjoy your precious pet-friendly gardens!

THE
Pet-Friendly Garden

First published 2000 by Pan Books, an imprint of
Macmillan General Books
25 Eccleston Place,
London SW1W 9NF
Basingstoke and Oxford

Associated companies throughout the world

www.macmillan.co.uk

ISBN 0 330 39316 2

9 8 7 6 5 4 3 2 1

A CIP catalogue record for this book is available from the British Library.

Designed and produced for Macmillan General Books by:

BCS Publishing Ltd,
Temple Court,
109 Oxford Road,
Oxford OX4 2ER

Colour Reproduction by: Aylesbury Studios, Bromley, Kent

Printed and bound in Great Britain by:
Bath Press

Contents

Introduction *by Richard Barrett*

Ten years ago, my wife and I acquired our first puppy, had our first new baby and bought a new house with our first real garden – all in a short space of time. To describe that minute back yard as a garden is a gross exaggeration, but we were intent on making it into something special. Being an active spaniel, the puppy had other ideas, and soon turned the postage stamp of a lawn to mud, which was trodden all through the house. Fighting disappointment, we searched gardening books and magazines for ideas to help us solve our problem. Needless to say we found little advice other than how to scare cats out of your garden, and how to keep pets off your flowerbeds. It is perhaps ironic that you only have to change the order of two letters and 'pets' becomes 'pest'. This sadly sums up the prevailing attitude in most publications. We pressed on regardless, replacing the lawn with paving, and protecting plants in raised beds and containers. Livia, the puppy, was happy, and so were we.

Five years later, I joined Pet Plan, the world's largest pet insurance specialists, and got to know some amazing statistics. There are 6 million dogs and 8 million cats in the UK and 57 million dogs and 80 million cats in the US, and one of the main leisure interests of people with pets is gardening. In fact, the majority of people owning a dog have a garden. So why are there no books on garden design for all these enthusiasts who love their pets as well as loving their gardens? The next year we got together with Blue Cross, one of the UK's leading animal charities, and set about creating a 'pet-friendly' garden as an exhibit at Hampton Court Palace flower show, the largest show of its kind in the world. Our goal was simple: we wanted to show how an ordinary back garden or yard could be designed to satisfy the needs of the gardener as well as their pet. We never realized just how much interested we would generate. An approach from Steve McCurdy of BCS Publishing and the enthusiasm of Macmillan led to this book, and to the creation of two further 'pet-friendly' gardens for inclusion in it: one suitable for a small urban back yard, and one for a larger rural setting.

The three specially designed gardens are intended to inspire keen beginners and more seasoned gardeners alike. The designs include pet-friendly garden features that can easily be constructed by any competent DIY householder using commonly available materials. The book also contains many other tips for making your garden enjoyable and safe for yourself and your pet. If reading it encourages you to adopt some of the ideas in your own garden, it will have achieved its modest ambitions. Should it help any pet-hating gardener to live in peaceful coexistence with cats and dogs, I will be well satisfied.

My thanks are due to everyone who helped and encouraged me along the way, particularly Patsy Bloom, David Simpson and George Stratford of Pet Plan Ltd for allowing me to indulge my personal interest; Alan Kennard and his colleagues at the Blue Cross for their support and enthusiasm; Pat McCann of Merrist Wood College for helping me to get started; Clare Palgrave and Jacquie Gordon for their commitment to the idea and for designing such great gardens; the Royal Horticultural Society for softening up and allowing pets into the show gardens we created; all the pet owners and veterinary surgeons who readily shared their ideas; the team at Pet Plan simply for coping with excessive enthusiasm; my Mum and Dad for being the first gardeners in my life; long-time friend Richard McCaie, who lit my gardening fuse; my wife and children, Cindy, Eleanor and Jolyon; our darling spaniels, Laura and Spice, and our rabbits, Houdy and Helly.

Caring for your pet's needs

Understanding your pet's behaviour is important; it will help you make your garden a pet-friendly environment, as well as a garden that you are able to enjoy. Your choice of pet will depend on your personal inclinations, the size of your garden and the amount of time you can spend looking after a pet. If you are unable to be at home during the day and you lead a busy life, a cat will be a more sensible choice than a dog. However, you might also consider a rabbit or a tortoise.

THE URBAN TIGER

The urban tiger. Just like its near relatives, the lions and tigers, this blue cream shorthair attentively stalks its prey.

Cats have been domestic pets ever since the Egyptians first used them for controlling vermin in their grain stores over 3,000 years ago. However, despite this long association with humans, cats have never given up their independence, coming and going as they wish, and asking for little more than a small supply of food. Even today, the domestic cat is not far removed from some of the world's most dangerous predators. Your cat may appear to be a perfect companion that bears little resemblance to a tiger, but it is still highly independent and will only share your house and garden on its own terms.

While both dogs and cats are meat-eaters, a well-fed dog will seldom waste much energy hunting, although it may enjoy a brief chase after a rabbit. Like their ancestors the wolves, dogs prefer to hunt in packs so that they can improve the chances of a successful kill.

Cats are the exact opposite. Although lions may hunt in prides, most wild cats hunt for their food alone. The domestic cat is the same. Despite years of domestication, cats are still superbly elegant, highly efficient hunters. Even a plump and lazy cat that spends most of the day sleeping in a favourite warm spot in the house will be transformed out in the garden, intently observing a bird. At such times cats show much of the primeval instincts of a leopard or a jaguar. No matter how well you feed your cat, or how much you dislike it when

your cat presents you with the remains of a kill, there is little you can do to stop this behaviour.

Observing your cat's behaviour will give you plenty of ideas about designing your garden to cater for its instinctive needs. In fact, if you provide a number of features that allow your cat to satisfy its instincts in your garden, it may be less prone to wander. For instance, cats have good eyesight and like to rest in places where they can survey their territory for potential prey or intruders. This means they prefer a high vantage point in the sun, where they are safe from danger themselves. You will frequently find your cat on top of a wall or a shed, basking in the sun, but always ready for action at the sight of a dog or a neighbour's cat entering its territory.

When they are resting, cats prefer a high vantage point from which they can keep one eye on their territory. The local birdlife might not always agree with their choice of perch, however!

When your cat gets the urge to hunt, it will seek out places where it can lurk in readiness for possible prey. Ideally, cats want lots of dense undergrowth and long grass in which to hide and stalk. If all you offer is a patio and bare vertical walls, the chances are that your cat will be off over the wall to somewhere better suited for hunting. To help prevent your cat from killing small rodents and birds, you can fit a bell on its collar to warn these garden visitors of your cat's whereabouts. This certainly helps, but does not always work. Many cats manage a kill despite having a bell fitted.

If you wish to encourage birds into your garden, you should only provide food in places where your cat has little chance of catching them. This means hanging out seed-holders for tits and finches where your cat cannot reach them, and making bird-tables inaccessible to your cat. You can buy bird-tables and bowls that can be suspended at the ends of long branches, making it very difficult for a stalking cat to pounce on an unsuspecting victim. If you have a pedestal bird-table that your cat tries to scale, place a piece of plastic piping over the stake. It is a talented cat that is able to climb a smooth-sided pipe.

Territorial claims

Like their wild relatives, cats are social animals. Allowed out into the local neighbourhood, they will quickly establish their position in the pecking order of the local cat community. This is usually dominated by the strongest tom cat, with positions determined by trials of strength. Surprisingly, these top cats rarely have the largest harems, and are not automatic choices for breeding queens. Instead, it seems that hierarchies are based on having access to food; the dominant tom frequently exercises control over the largest territory.

Cats are territorial by nature, and will fight to defend their plot against an intruder at all times. If there are a lot of cats in your neighbourhood, your cat's territory may be little more than your own garden, but if there is no cat next door, your cat will probably regard that garden as part of its territory. If you own a number of cats, they will share the territory and will all help to defend it against intruders. Where there are few cats, a dominant tom may have a large territory and regard all the neighbouring gardens as its own.

Enthusiastic gardeners with no cat of their own frequently see such toms (and indeed any alien cat) as a complete nuisance, and will go to great lengths to prevent cats from entering their gardens. They might resort to chemical deterrents, sophisticated devices such as sonic cat scarers, or even lion dung. Who knows what nightmare visions come into the mind of the humble moggie that picks up the scent of the king of the jungle in its own backyard? A cat is often the best deterrent against other cats, however. So, if you do not have a cat, perhaps you should consider getting one.

Cats are territorial by nature, even if they are only defending a seat in the sun.

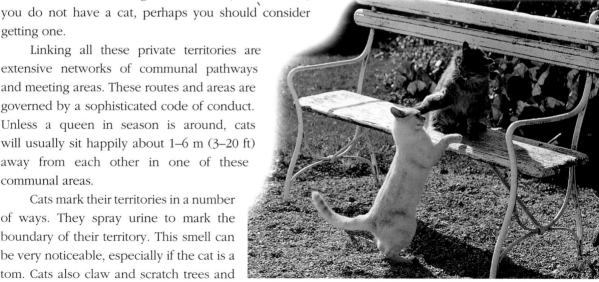

Linking all these private territories are extensive networks of communal pathways and meeting areas. These routes and areas are governed by a sophisticated code of conduct. Unless a queen in season is around, cats will usually sit happily about 1–6 m (3–20 ft) away from each other in one of these communal areas.

Cats mark their territories in a number of ways. They spray urine to mark the boundary of their territory. This smell can be very noticeable, especially if the cat is a tom. Cats also claw and scratch trees and fences. Not only does this leave a visual marker to indicate their territory, but it also leaves a scent deposited from the sweat glands in the paw-pads. Cats also deposit scent from their sebaceous glands by rubbing their heads and faces against low objects.

Cats need claws for hunting, climbing and protecting themselves against other aggressive cats. They keep them in good condition by scratching at rough surfaces such as tree-trunks, fences or posts. This keeps the claws free of debris like dead skin, and helps them shed the outer layer of the old dead claw to expose the new growing tip underneath. If you look hard, you can sometimes find the older, outer layer of claw embedded in your damaged tree-trunk.

Dealing with cat marking

There is much that you can do to accommodate your cat's need to mark. Avoid planting conifers on prominent corners where they may be regularly sprayed with feline urine and are likely to end up brown and withered. Similarly, if you plant ornamental trees with wonderful textured bark in an open position, do not be surprised if they become damaged by scratching. You should either protect the trunk with chicken wire or relocate the tree to a less prominent spot before it grows too large to move easily.

By far the best way to deal with spraying and scratching, however, is to provide for it. This may be as simple as putting low posts round the garden. They will rapidly become favourite marking and scratching posts for your cat and the bark of your ornamental tree should escape further attention. If your cat persists in damaging a favourite tree, try to catch it in the act, hiss at it loudly and clap your hands. This is usually enough to stop the scratching. Never hit the cat or punish it. If the damage continues, you could ask your vet to trim the tips of your cat's claws, as this will help to minimize the damage. If you become really desperate, discuss with your vet whether you should have your cat declawed. This practice is common in the US, where many cats are kept indoors, but is less common in the UK, where most vets consider it cruel and unnecessary.

DOG BREEDS AND NEEDS

Because dog breeds have been developed for certain skills and behaviours, there is probably no such animal as the average dog. When you think about making your garden dog-friendly, it is

Because most owners *only tend to keep a single dog, it is easy to forget they are natural pack animals with a dominant pack leader. Here a group of dogs show typical pack behaviour, reasserting leadership position.*

important to consider the specific characteristics and typical behaviour of your breed. You might have read all about the breed before you brought your dog home. If not, it is well worth doing so now. By understanding where the breed originated and what it was used for, you will be able to tailor the garden accordingly. Breeds such as the greyhound, Saluki, Afghan and borzoi are capable of running at high speeds over short distances, for example, and the design of your garden should reflect that. Small dogs may have difficulty with high steps; a Newfoundland will appreciate a plunge pool on hot summer days; a terrier may find digging flowerbeds irresistible if left to its own devices; an agile dog may be able to scale a 2-m (6.6-ft) fence, and so on.

Home guard

Whatever breed of dog you have, it is still a domesticated pack animal. Dogs will protect you and your home because they are social animals. Wild dogs and wolves live and hunt in packs with a dominant leader. In the absence of a pack and pack leader, the household members become the pack and the head of the household typically becomes the pack leader. The house and garden are your dog's territory, and it will have strong instincts to protect and guard you, the rest of the household, the home and the garden.

All dogs (other than the basenji) can bark, and even little dogs can deter burglars. Their senses of smell and hearing are much more sensitive than those of humans, and any unfamiliar noise or scent can set them howling at any time of day or night. If you want to enhance your dog's ability as a watchdog or guard dog, try putting gravel on all your paths and below all your windows. The lightest footstep will produce a crunch that will be picked up by all but the most insensitive canine ears.

Dogs are social animals and in the wild would require the company of their pack to be happy. It is not surprising then that the domesticated dog is interested in all activities and wants to be with a member of the household all the time. Left alone, dogs can become stressed or bored, and may be destructive both in the house and the garden. A bored dog can soon open up a crater in the middle of your favourite flowerbed. Alternatively, it may decide that life is more interesting over the garden fence and be intent on escape. Nobody can live happily with an unruly dog, so if you take the trouble to train your pet, you will be doing both of you a favour. The dog will be easier to live with and your garden will look the better for it.

Territorial instincts

If you establish yourself as the pack leader, your dog will accept that you are responsible for the defence of the pack. If you welcome another human or canine stranger without any show of aggression, your dog will be quite content to let them into your home and into the pack's territory. However, in your absence, your dog will take over this role. If anyone comes through the front gate when you are not on hand, the dog is likely to defend its territory. If the intruder

*A **Dalmatian** lies across the doorway, ready to raise the alarm if a stranger appears.*

retreats, your dog will be happy that it has done its duty and protected the pack's territory. Postmen, in particular, are apt to become the victims of this protective behaviour. In fact, the dog may even come to recognize the postman's uniform as a signal that this is someone it can chase. When the postman retreats, it reinforces the dog's behaviour.

You can tackle this problem by being on hand to meet all visitors and clearly demonstrate to your dog that you, as pack leader, are happy to meet them. Alternatively, you may decide that it is better to restrict your dog to the back garden and let visitors get to the front door unmolested. This also means that you do not have to worry about them forgetting to close the front gate.

A dog's sense of smell is thought to be one million times more sensitive than that of a human. It has a large sensory area in its nose that is densely packed with sensory cells. This sends information to the brain, where the dog has 40 times more brain cells involved in scent recognition than a human. Faced with any new experience, humans look and listen; dogs smell.

Like cats, dogs use smell to mark their territory. Male dogs do this by cocking a leg and urinating frequently. Female dogs also do this, but less obviously. Because your dog is competing with other neighbourhood dogs, it will try to leave its scent as frequently and as effectively as possible on any suitable object. For a male dog this means cocking its leg and urinating as high as it can so that its scent is at nose-height and is less likely to be washed off by the next passing dog. You cannot stop your dog from doing this, and it is futile to try and do so.

Instead of letting your male dog scald your favourite shrubs and conifers with streams of hot urine, it is better to provide some scenting posts round the garden. Your dog is likely to use them in preference to anything else, and your plants will no longer be scorched. Because bitches squat to urinate, they will prefer to use your lawn, if you have one, and this can result in patches of burnt grass. You can follow your bitch around with a bucket of water to dilute the urine as soon as it is passed, but unless you are particularly diligent, there is bound to be some damage to the lawn.

Dogs and bitches also make scent marks by scratching the ground with their hindlegs and kicking up any loose earth. This deposits scent from glands in the paws. So do not be surprised when your dog starts to scratch your lawn to shreds, leaving bare patches

all over it. If you have a large expanse of lawn, you can probably put
up with this behaviour. However, if you only have a small patch and
a dog that is larger than a toy breed, your lawn is likely to be ruined
quite quickly. In the long term the easiest solution is to do away with
the lawn altogether.

EASY-CARE RABBITS

Fewer households nowadays have someone at home during the day, so families are finding it increasingly difficult to keep a dog as their chosen pet. Instead, some people compromise and choose a cat or a rabbit. However you come to own a rabbit, you are one of an increasing number of rabbit owners. Rabbits make ideal pets for busy people, particularly adults. You do not have to take them for walks, they are easy to feed and, because they are crepuscular (active at dawn and dusk and resting during the day), they are ready for action when you get home from work.

Because your rabbit spends much of its time in a hutch or, if it is a house-rabbit, in the home, you may think you do not need to understand its behaviour. However, understanding your rabbit's needs will enable you to give it a happier, stress-free life.

Prey animals

Unlike cats and dogs, which are natural hunters, rabbits are prey, and this accounts for much of their behaviour. Prey animals do not show obvious signs of fear, pain or contentment. In the wild, such behaviour could cost them their lives because it attracts attention and may also indicate that they are vulnerable or not alert to the presence of a predator.

The concern not to end up as someone else's meal shows itself in all aspects of a rabbit's life. It spends most of the daylight hours underground in complete darkness, preferring to feed, court and play during the safer hours of darkness. Because of this, sight is not as important to them as smell, and every rabbit has an individual scent profile that plays a key role in its communication with other rabbits. A rabbit marks its territory by leaving secretions from its chin gland on prominent objects around it and on other rabbits. As with cats and dogs, urine and faeces are also important territorial markers.

House or hutch

As people realize that rabbits can make good companions, and can be house-trained easily, many are taken into the home as house-rabbits. Those that are not are often confined to hutches, many of which are far too small for their health and happiness. Rabbits need to be able to stretch to their full length and height, and also to be able to run and jump. In a small hutch, where they are unable to exercise, they are likely to become bored, depressed and overweight.

As long as you stay with them at all times, rabbits can be let out to explore your garden. You should check that you do not have any poisonous plants anywhere, and should keep an eye out for dogs and cats.

If they become overweight, they are less able to groom themselves and, in the heat of a small hutch, the likelihood of fly-strike increases during the summer months. Fly-strike is when flies lay their eggs in the soiled coat of an old, ill, injured or overweight rabbit that is unable to groom itself. The resulting infestation of maggots does not stop at the surface. They frequently burrow into sound flesh, producing toxins that create a state of shock and sometimes death. The answer to such problems is simple. Provide the biggest hutch and run you are able to, and be fastidious in cleaning it out.

Preventing disease

No matter where you live, you should ensure that your rabbit is vaccinated every year against two potentially fatal viral diseases: myxomatosis and viral haemorrhagic disease. The latter is a particularly nasty disease, where the rabbit

Most rabbit hutches are simply too small for the rabbit's health and happiness. Even if you have a small garden, you should still try to provide your rabbit with ample accommodation, perhaps by building a multi-storey hutch like this.

becomes severely ill with internal bleeding in the lungs, gut and urinary tract. Death usually occurs very quickly; in many cases the rabbit is simply found dead in the hutch. Both diseases are spread by insects, fleas or direct contact with an infected rabbit. If you live near any countryside, your rabbit may be visited by wild rabbits and touch noses with them through the wire. Even a rabbit that lives permanently indoors is by no means safe.

One rabbit or more?

There are few generalizations that can safely be applied to rabbits. But one truth remains unchallenged: rabbits are not meant to live in solitude. Like humans and many other creatures, wild rabbits live in social groups. A community or warren may number a hundred individuals working together to create, maintain and peacefully share a network of tunnels. They co-operate to find food, watch for and warn off predators, and raise their young.

This need for companionship can be partially met by a human, but once you have lived with a bonded pair, you will know that even the most devoted human does not quite fit the bill. Bonded pairs are rarely out of each other's sight. Rabbits interact constantly, not so much with sounds as with movements. Sometimes they will nudge one another, demanding to be groomed, or chase each other round their run. At other times their communications will be less obvious, being no more than slight shifts in position, twitches or patterns of breathing. You can sense some of this quiet conversation by lying down beside two talkative rabbits.

Fortunately for everyone involved, what is good for a rabbit is also good for its owner. Pairs are much easier to care for, get into less trouble and tend to relate better to people. Boredom and depression are common symptoms of loneliness. These can be accompanied by destructiveness and hyperactivity in some rabbits, especially the smaller breeds, and withdrawal in others.

Rabbits are social animals and are not meant to live solitary lives. Single rabbits tend to become bored and depressed, whereas bonded pairs are in constant communication.

Choosing a pair

Unless you are intent on breeding, unneutered rabbits of opposite sexes should never be put together. In addition to preventing an unwanted litter, neutering makes for smooth introductions and better long-term relationships between same-sex partners as well as male/female pairs. Nor should you house more than one male with a single female, or two males where they can smell an unneutered female. It is often said that a rabbit and a guinea pig make a good pairing. In practice this is rarely true, as the rabbit tends to harrass and dominate the guinea pig. Each would be happier with one of its own species.

It is sometimes said that you should let your rabbit choose its own companion. This would involve taking it to a breeder or a rescue centre and trying it out with a few potential companions. There is a risk that your rabbit will pick up a disease, but if all the rabbits involved are healthy, the risk is small.

Introducing two rabbits requires planning and supervision, as the pairing is as likely to result in dramatic hostility as it is to result in lifelong devotion. Once through the introductory phase, a bonded pair will usually become devoted to each other, so much so that care must be taken when one rabbit dies. However, bereaved rabbits often accept a new friend more readily than a rabbit that has never had a partner – a tribute to their resilience and their sociability.

The best way to introduce two rabbits is on neutral territory, which neither has had time to scent-mark. Never put a male or female into another female's territory as they will fight. The process starts with putting the two rabbits next to each other in cages so that they can investigate each other through the bars. If they appear to get on, gradually try putting them together. A water pistol is handy for stopping any fighting.

It is generally very easy to recognize when your rabbit has made up its mind and chosen its companion. You will find that you get much more enjoyment from having two rabbits living together, and your garden will be alive with the sound of their play. You can also rest assured that you no longer have a bored, depressed rabbit sealed in solitary confinement at the bottom of the garden.

A rabbit and a tortoise bask on a sunny lawn. As days become cooler, a tortoise will bask less, eat less, and tend to stay in one place, signalling that it is ready to hibernate.

Venerable tortoises

Some tortoises are known to live for 60–80 years, and many may live for even longer. Because growth varies with the availability of food, tortoises grow faster in captivity. This makes it almost impossible to determine the exact age of an adult tortoise. In order to protect endangered tortoises, it is now illegal to import some species into the United Kingdom. If buying a tortoise in the UK, it is advisable to obtain a captive-bred animal through a reputable breeding society. In the United States, tortoises are bred in captivity, though wild desert tortoises are still widely available in western states.

Unless they are hibernating, tortoises must be kept outdoors in as large an area as you can provide. If possible, give them the run of your entire garden or yard, making sure that it is escape-proof and that the tortoise cannot inadvertently fall into a pond or pool. You must also be sure that any other pets, such as dogs or cats, will not harm the tortoise. Get rid of all poisonous plants and do not use chemical pesticides or fertilizers.

It is cruel to tether a tortoise by a leg or through a hole drilled in the shell. If you have to restrict its range, confine it to a run, or dig

an outdoor terrarium for it. This is no more than a steep-sided pit that is ecape-proof, but is large enough to prevent the tortoise from destroying the grass. The terrarium should also have some large evergreen shrubs to provide shade from the hot sun and shelter from the rain. Tortoises spend most of their time under thick vegetation such as bushes; alternatively they can shelter in a waterproof box provided by you. As long as a tortoise has adequate shelter from the sun and cold, and a place to retire to on cool nights, it will be happy.

Know your tortoise

It is important that you get to know the normal behaviour of your tortoise, because changes in behaviour are often the first sign of illness. Tortoises are very susceptible to respiratory ailments. Warning signs are a runny nose, loss of appetite and gasping. Respiratory disease can often be cured if treatment is begun immediately, so consult your veterinary surgeon as soon as there is any sign of illness.

As the days become cooler (usually during October in Britain) tortoises will begin to go into hibernation. They will eat less, bask less and will tend to stay in one place. Depending on the temperature of the region, tortoises hibernate from October to March. In some parts of the world they may not hibernate at all. In warmer climates, tortoises may hibernate outside. However, you need to consider the location of their burrow or nest. If there is a significant risk of flooding from rainfall, do not allow your pet to hibernate there. In more temperate climates, tortoises should be stored somewhere cool, like a garage, where the temperature does not rise above 15°C (60°F). Place the tortoise in a sturdy cardboard box that is deep enough to prevent it climbing out. Cover the tortoise with insulating layers of newspaper, or half fill the box with hay. The box is best placed off the floor in an area that is free from draughts or rats.

A hibernating tortoise should be checked periodically. It will usually respond if its foot is touched. If the tortoise should wake, encourage it to return to sleep. In the spring, when the days begin to

warm up, the tortoise will become active in its storage box. Give it a warm bath, paying particular attention to its eyelids, which may be glued together. The tortoise will often take a long, steady drink. Within a week or two it should resume its normal activities of eating, exercising and sunbathing.

It is important that a tortoise is plump and in good health before it begins hibernating, otherwise it may not survive the winter. By the end of the summer a well-fed tortoise will have formed fat reserves round its shoulders and legs. If your tortoise appears to be sick or injured in any way, do not allow it to hibernate, and immediately take it to your vet. To stop a tortoise hibernating, bring it indoors and keep it at 24°–29°C (75°–85°F). It will require space for exercising and regular feedings.

Tortoise food

Tortoises are vegetarians and thrive on a variety of greens, fruit and grains. In the wild, tortoises eat cereal grasses, seasonal flowers and plants. In captivity they will flourish on grass, dandelions, clover and almost anything else they can get at, particularly green vegetables and fruit. Tortoises have a high calcium requirement, so occasionally sprinkle crushed calcium tablets on their food, or offer them crushed, boiled eggshells. All fresh fruits and vegetables must be washed, and no chemicals should be used on the plants and grass in your garden.

You should provide a shallow dish of water at all times so that your tortoise can drink and bathe at will. A margarine-tub lid is ideal. If you provide suitable food and water, and occasionally wipe its shell with some olive oil, your tortoise should have a long and healthy life.

Tortoises as fashion accessory

Because of the ban on importing certain species of tortoises into the United Kingdom, tortoises have become very sought-after and fashionable pets there. However, it is unlikely that tortoises will ever regain the standing they enjoyed in some parts of British society in the first half of the 20th century.

A pair of tortoises enjoying their first meal after coming out of hibernation.

Christina Foyle, a member of the family who established one of London's largest and most famous bookshops, was addicted to animals of all kinds. She enjoyed holding lavish parties for publishers and writers at the family's 12th-century home. Her guests always worried about whether her peacocks would damage their expensive cars as they pecked at their reflections in the shining chrome and paintwork. On summer nights, visitors were said to be bemused by the lights that moved slowly around the large garden. If they had made a closer inspection, they would have found that these were candles attached to the backs of Christina Foyle's many tortoises.

GENTLE GUINEA PIGS

Unlike rabbits, which can deliver a painful kick and a bite to demonstrate their discontent, guinea pigs are peaceful animals and often make better pets for small children. They can be housed individually, or in a group with other guinea pigs, as long as some simple rules are observed.

Males that have been born and raised together may be kept together. However, if a male is separated from a group for more than a few hours, he should not be returned because it will cause a fight.

Guinea pigs can be kept together as long as a few basic rules are observed. They are more gentle than rabbits, so can make better pets for children.

Nor should you try to introduce a new male into a group with other males. Females do not usually fight, but when you introduce a new female to a group, observe them closely to make sure there are no scuffles. Guinea pigs should not be kept with other species such as rabbits. Not only do they have different nutritional requirements, they frequently cause each other unnecessary stress.

Although guinea pigs can be housed outdoors in much the same way as rabbits, they are much more susceptible to temperature extremes, and should be kept at 20°–22°C (68°–72°F). This means that, in a temperate climate, they will need well-insulated winter accommodation inside a shed.

Guinea pig pellets are formulated to meet the particular nutritional needs of guinea pigs and are high in vitamin C. But to make sure that your guinea pig gets enough vitamins, you should supplement the prepared pellets with fresh vegetables and fruits, making sure that the feed bowl and water bowl are never empty.

DECORATIVE DOVES

If you would like more unusual pets, you could try keeping doves. Far from being quiet, gentle birds, doves are constantly active. If you take the time to study them, each will reveal an individual character, and you will soon come to recognize each bird and want to give them names. Males constantly display before any available female, eventually pairing, and then fighting their way up the pecking order to establish themselves in a vacant nest-box; the top birds take the highest bay facing the sun. All this courtship and rivalry means that dovecotes are busy, noisy places.

Prolific breeders

A bonded pair will court and mate, producing two eggs that they dutifully take turns to sit on until they hatch 18–19 days after laying. After the first two weeks, the young reach what is known as the 'squeaker' stage, because of the constant noise they make demanding food. Both parents feed the young on pigeon's milk (an easily digested custard produced in their crops). By the time the young are

A small dovecote and a few pairs of doves can be an attractive addition to a country garden, but you should ensure it does not get overcrowded.

three to four weeks old, they are able to feed themselves, and the parents are ready to start breeding again. Often the next clutch of eggs is produced before the young have flown.

If you intend to bring charm to a country garden with two or three pairs, be careful. They can quickly multiply and become uncontrollable, unless their progress is checked. In medieval times, this meant taking the young squabs before they could fly and eating them. Unless you have a liking for pigeon pie, today it means removing their eggs before your dovecote becomes overrun.

Designing the garden

N ot all pet owners have homes with extensive gardens, but this need not prevent the creation of a pet-friendly environment. There is much that can be done to make even a small garden stimulating and entertaining for dogs, cats, rabbits and other pets, while ensuring that it remains a joy for you and your family. However, in order to create the perfect environment, you must consider certain basic questions. How can you keep your pet safely within your garden? What does it need to remain happy and occupied? How can you best cope with your pet's natural toilet habits? What plants are suitable for the pet-friendly garden?

It should be possible to plan a garden that provides recreation and relaxation for everyone. In addition to attractive planting and seating areas for humans, a range of features such as play tunnels for dogs and viewing platforms for cats should cater for the behavioural needs of pets. Water features and shady bowers will appeal to all users. Start by following the step-by-step plan on pages 28–29.

A West Highland terrier rests in the entrance to its garden (opposite). The paved surface can easily be washed down with a hosepipe, using a mild disinfectant that is not harmful to animals or to plants.

GARDEN BOUNDARIES

An important consideration when planning a pet-friendly garden is what type of boundary you will need. Your requirements will vary depending on your pet, your neighbours, your proximity to a busy road, the size of your garden and your need for privacy.

Dog-proof barriers

Before you even consider bringing a new puppy or dog home, you should erect a wall or fencing around your house and garden and make sure that it is totally secure. Put simply, that means your dog should not be able to get through it, over it or under it. Do not think that you can wait until your puppy is allowed out into the garden by itself; you are likely to find that it has slipped out of the front door behind a visitor's legs and is out in the street where it can easily cause an accident.

Do not skimp and cut corners by erecting a barrier that is only just high enough. Your puppy may not be able to clear a low fence, but when it is fully grown, it will be a different matter. Faced with an attraction such as a bitch in season on the other side of the fence, even a small dog can clear considerable heights. Scaling 2 m (6.6 ft) or more is not uncommon for larger breeds. Large breeds are also heavy, and an energetic breed such as a German shepherd can soon break through a weak fence. It is better to be safe than sorry. If your next-door neighbour also has a dog, you may find it better to erect a solid fence rather than use wire. If they are unable to see a potential rival, most dogs will be much quieter.

Surrounding a small garden with a high wall or a solid fence can make it look more like a prison exercise yard than a garden. There

STEP-BY-STEP GARDEN DESIGN

1. Make a wish-list
Begin by listing everything you think your pets would enjoy in a garden, then think about who else will be using it. Adults may want somewhere to relax and entertain; children may want a play area. Is anyone an avid plant collector? Will anyone be growing plants from seed?

2. Remember the essentials
Do not forget to assign a place to items such as dustbins, the washing line, or the garden shed in your garden.

3. Choose an appropriate style
Visit gardens and browse through books and magazines to collect examples of the style you would like to achieve. Remember that the final result will look better if it fits in with the style of your house and uses some of the same materials.

4. Measure up the garden
Measure your space as precisely as you can, remembering to check the diagonals: few gardens are perfectly rectangular. Draw up your plan on squared paper. Use pencil at first, until you are happy that the plan is reasonably accurate. Plot any existing features, locating their position by taking two or more measurements from fixed points.

5. Identify any important vistas
Are there any views that you would like to see from your garden? Or do you have some eyesores that you would prefer to hide? Most of the time you will view your garden from the house, so take a long look at it from each of the main windows. Work out how to add features to improve the view, or how to screen objects such as the heating oil tank with planting or trellis.

6. Locate the sunny and the shady areas
Either by using a compass to locate north, or by observing your garden at different times of the day, work out which areas get sun and which remain in shade. Knowing this will help you choose plants that will thrive in each area.

are several ways of overcoming this. Covering the structure with big, bold masses of planting material will help soften it, especially if you include some trees and shrubs that grow above the height of the fence or wall. Fencing that has a strong horizontal pattern, such as slatted screens, will visually counter some of the height. Different heights and types of fencing will also give a more pleasing result.

Fencing that allows you to see through it, such as palings or a trellis, will make a small space seem larger, especially if it allows you an attractive view beyond your boundary. Such fencing also provides good support for climbers. These can be chosen for their seasonal colour or, if you prefer, to provide an evergreen screen to give you privacy. If you choose open fencing, you will need to make sure that your pet cannot

***Plotting a design on squared paper** is the easiest way of planning your garden, using the steps below.*

7. Develop your plan

Begin by sketching in the hard landscaping, such as paths and patios, and any large areas, such as a lawn. Try to keep to simple, strong shapes that hold the design together, adding beds and finer detail later. You can vary heights round the garden with raised beds, terraces and decking.

In a large garden, applying the 'rule of thirds' will help you to achieve a harmonious design. The third of the garden surrounding the house is kept formal, using regular shapes. The third of the garden furthest from the house is the least restrained, and is allowed to blend into the surrounding countryside. The middle third acts as a bridge between the other two.

In a smaller, urban garden, it may be best to base the entire garden on the repetition of a single regular shape, with the different areas of the garden having a very simple relationship to each other. To do this, divide your plan into a grid of no more than 30 squares. Cut out a number of pieces of card in your chosen shape. This may be a square or a rectangle that covers a

number of your grid squares. Some pieces of card can be the same size, while others can be half the size. Play around with the shapes on your plan. Try overlapping them, or even turning them through 45 degrees to the boundaries, as this can help break up the boxiness of a small garden. Whatever you choose to do, the dimensions of each part of the garden will always be proportional to each other and to the overall dimensions of the garden. You do not have to stick to rectangles and squares; circles and ellipses are regular too.

8. Add the planting

Now you can add the planting, starting with the main structural plants and the trees and shrubs that will be the principal features. Detailed discussion of planting and plant lists can be found in Chapter 3.

squeeze through the gaps between the uprights or get underneath the fence.

In addition to jumping, your dog may be able to escape in other ways. Many hounds, such as beagles, and most of the terrier breeds are excellent diggers, and can tunnel beneath fences with remarkable speed. The only sure solution is to surround the garden completely with walling, but this is a costly exercise. Building a low wall and topping it with timber fencing is a cheaper solution. Wire fencing is cheaper still, but you will need to bury it well into the soil. As long as the bottom of the barrier is totally secure, you can get away with a less sturdy structure for the top part of the fence.

Trellis on top of a low brick wall makes a more than adequate barrier; it is highly unlikely that any dog will launch itself at it. You can cover the trellis with climbers, such as clematis and pyracantha. Trellis is also a good burglar deterrent as no sensible thief will risk scaling a structure that he knows is liable to collapse beneath him, especially if it is covered with a thorny climber.

If you have a large garden, or need to have a high fence, your budget may limit you to wire mesh. Galvanized or plastic-coated wire mesh strung between metal posts is relatively cheap and will last for many years with little maintenance. The only

Large mesh fencing *like this will be fine when they are fully grown, but in the meantime these Brittany spaniel puppies could easily escape.*

downside is that it is not the most attractive backdrop to a garden, so it would be best to screen it with hedging. If you back on to open land and are not too concerned about how the fence looks from the outside, a single row of hedging planted inside the wire will soon supply a screen. Otherwise, make a wire sandwich by planting one row of hedging outside the wire and another row inside the wire. There is no reason why you should choose the same species inside and out. A hardy, quick-growing species, such as laurel, might be ideal for outside the wire, while a flowering hedge will be attractive inside the wire. Remember to inspect the wire regularly for holes or weaknesses. This is much easier if you leave a narrow alley that you can comfortably squeeze along between one row of planting and the wire.

There are electronic methods of keeping pets contained, the most popular being marketed as the 'Freedom Fence'. A wire is laid around the perimeter of the garden or chosen area, and is either buried a few centimetres in the ground, or attached to existing fencing. A transmitter sends out a continuous low-power, low-frequency radio signal along the wire, which effectively acts as an aerial. The pet wears a tiny battery-powered receiver on its collar that picks up a coded signal from the wire. If the pet comes within 3 m (10 ft) of the wire, it hears a continuous warning bleep from the receiver. If it ignores the signal, as it may well do at the beginning, and continues up to the hidden wire, it will receive a small static shock, similar to the discharge you can get from a car door handle or a lift button. This will give the pet a surprise, but does not cause any pain. Most pets quickly get the idea.

Compared with the cost of enclosing a large garden with fencing, this technology is remarkably cheap. It can also solve many design problems. For instance, if you live in the country and there is a magnificent view beyond your garden, you could use it to create a modern-day ha-ha (a ditch or vertical drop, often containing a fence, that forms a barrier without interrupting the view). There would be no fence, hedge or observable barrier of any kind, and your garden would simply continue into the countryside beyond your boundary.

However, an electronic barrier is not always the perfect solution. It will stop your pet from venturing out, but will not prevent other pets and livestock from coming in. Dogs also need to be reasonably well trained. If your dog shows aggression or any signs of having an unreliable temperament when it comes into contact with other animals or people, you may have problems. Anxious to respond to the stimulus of someone or something within its sight, its speed and momentum may carry it over the hidden wire before it responds to the warning signal or the discharge.

With a little thought, even the most functional fence can be made attractive. This trellis panel separates the front and rear gardens, allowing visitors easy access to the house while keeping pets safely enclosed.

SURFACE VARIETY

Gardens can have several different kinds of surface. A large garden nearly always has a lawn, while a small garden may only have paving or decking. It is also worth considering areas of gravel or bark chippings. If you have a large garden, a mixture of surfaces will add interest and texture.

Lawn care

Trying to maintain an attractive lawn in a small garden that is shared with an active dog is an uphill battle – and one that is probably best conceded early on. In wet weather the lawn will be reduced to a quagmire. In a hot summer, even if you are using the most hard-wearing lawn seed, it is likely to be bare. Added to this, if your dog uses the lawn as somewhere to urinate, the lawn will scorch and become unsightly in the summer. You can run around after the dog with a watering can to dilute the concentrated urine, but this is perhaps not the most fulfilling activity. With some dedicated training, you can stop your dog from using the lawn as a toilet and encourage it to use another part of the garden. You could even have two lawns, one for humans and one hidden out the way that is specifically there for your dog. Although your dog will always want to be with you and will join in with what is happening on the family lawn, if it knows it should not use your lawn as a toilet, you will not expose yourselves to the risk of illness or infection.

Cats like grass, which is thought to be an aid to their digestion. As long as it has not been treated with chemicals, you should not be concerned if you see them eating it. Dogs also eat grass occasionally, although no one really knows why. If you do get rid of the lawn, a cat or dog will appreciate it if you keep a small patch of grass somewhere in the garden. It should be positioned so that it does not become part of a regular loop around the garden. If it does not get heavy wear, it can be kept longer and cut less frequently than normal.

Grass is the staple diet of rabbits. In fact, feeding them a diet that is not based on grass or hay is likely to result in health problems. In the wild, rabbits spend many hours each day devouring grasses. Not only does this provide them with most of the nourishment and roughage they require, it also keeps their teeth trim. A rabbit's teeth grow continually and, unless it is fed a diet that requires it to use them, the teeth can overgrow and protrude from the mouth. Overgrown teeth make it painful for a rabbit to eat, and sometimes it simply wastes away and dies. Left unchecked, the teeth may force their way up into the rabbit's nasal passage or eye socket. By the time this is detected, there is often little that can be done for the animal and euthanasia is the kindest option.

Brick paving and then *gravel separate the lawn from the house, adding interest to a well-used thoroughfare. Note that the gravel is also surrounded with a brick edging to stop it overflowing into the lawn and damaging the mower blades.*

One of the best ways to allow a rabbit access to grass is by getting a portable run that can be moved round an area of fresh, medium-length grass. Unless you have an orchard or a paddock, this is often difficult, especially in a small garden where the lawn is likely to be maintained with weedkillers and chemicals. Even if you have suitable grass, you should introduce your rabbit to it slowly, allowing it no more than 10 minutes' grazing on the first day, building up the time over a period of a week. Good-quality hay is a totally acceptable alternative, but you should make sure that it is fresh and sweet-smelling. Old hay tends to be low in calcium and can often be laden with mites and fungal spores. Your nose will tell you if the hay is off. You could also try your rabbit with commercially prepared, dried, fresh grass. It is made for feeding to horses and can be bought from agricultural feed merchants or good pet stores. So, even if you have a rabbit as a pet, you may decide to give up your lawn and replace the grass with some other material.

Hard surfaces

In addition to your pets, your garden will need to satisfy the needs of other people using it. Areas for entertaining may require a different surface from a play area, for example. Some of these may be hard, such as paving and decking, while others will be soft, such as gravel and bark. The surfacing material you choose for the different areas of your garden will depend upon the style, suitability and the cost of the material.

Timber decking has been used in the United States and Europe for centuries, and is steadily gaining popularity in the UK. Decking is useful for linking the house and garden, especially on a sloping site. In fact, when faced with such a situation, it is often the easiest way of creating a level space. Although decks made of hardwood need no preservative treatment and last for many years, the cost is frequently prohibitive. You should also make sure that the wood does not come from an endangered species. Softwood is nowhere near as hardy and needs planing to prevent splinters finding their way into a cat's or dog's feet.

Decking is increasingly popular, but it can be too slippery a surface for an older dog.

Even when the surface is machine-profiled to give it some texture, decking tends to become slippery in wet weather. In a temperate climate with a high rainfall, decking may be damp for most of the year. In Continental Europe and the US, which both have more extreme temperatures, a deck may be covered with snow in the winter, but has the opportunity to dry out thoroughly in the hotter summer months. So, while cats might live happily with decking, the surface can present a hazard to a small or older dog. Not only is a deck likely to be slippery for part of the year, it could also involve a flight of steps, which could be perilous for an infirm pet.

Paving has universal appeal, as it requires little maintenance and there is a wide choice of materials to

suit the mood and design of every garden. In rural areas, natural local stone, or a good imitation, is likely to be the most suitable choice. In urban gardens, almost anything might be possible, although it is always better if the material complements the local building style. As long as the material does not become slippery in rain or snow, your pet is not likely to complain. Paved areas, on which you might have a table and chairs for entertaining, can frequently become favourite places for dogs. They enjoy being with people, and love lounging on the warm paving. As long as the surface can be washed down easily, using a hosepipe and a mild disinfectant that is safe for animals and plants, and has a slight incline so that water does not stand on it, you should have few problems.

Mellowed brick *makes a safe and hardwearing path for a traditional cottage garden.*

Soft surfaces

Gravel and other softer materials such as bark and shingle are becoming more popular in gardens. They are cheap, easy to lay and add an extra dimension to the garden. In smaller gardens, where it is hardly worth maintaining a lawn the size of a postage-stamp, gravel is now commonly used. If your pet fouls a gravelled area, it can easily be washed down. Not only is gravel hard-wearing, if you use it as a mulch on beds and between planting, it helps to retain moisture. Gravel is an ideal medium to promote self-seeding, and will soon become colonized with young plants. Shrubs, bulbs and perennials will happily grow through a layer of gravel, as long as it is no more than 10 cm (4 in) thick. It is an ideal surface for paths and underneath windows, because it is noisy to walk on and will alert you and your dog to intruders.

Plants that tolerate *dry conditions,* *such as* Armeria maritima *(sea pink or thrift) will thrive in gravel.*

For pets, gravel is not all good news, however. It consists of natural rock chippings with sharp edges that can be thoroughly unpleasant for pets to walk on. River-washed shingle that has been rounded by the action of water, or sea-dredged pea shingle, may only be available in a limited range of colours, but it is more suitable for a garden with pets and children. Even then, you should choose a fine-textured, washed shingle in preference to larger pebbles, which a dog may still find unpleasant to walk on.

If you have ever walked across a pebble beach with bare feet, you will know exactly what your pet will be enduring.

Bark chippings are another form of soft surfacing. They can be laid under trees and planting, and give a natural feel to a garden. The bark eventually disintegrates and adds structure to the soil. Cats and dogs love bark as it retains many smells for them to investigate, and is fun to dig in. However, it can also be difficult to keep clear of pet waste, and is best avoided if there are young children around.

Safe steps

Not all gardens are perfectly flat. In fact, many of the most attractive gardens are located on sloping sites, where you can look down into areas of planting and up into the tops of trees. If your site is on a slope, even a gentle one, you will probably need to incorporate steps into your design. In a small garden this may involve no more than a couple of steps from outside the back door up on to the patio or the lawn; in a larger or more steeply sloping garden this may involve a more complex construction of a number of flat areas linked by steps. When you construct the steps, do consider how your pet will manage them, especially in its old age.

Just as many humans become arthritic as they age, so too do pets. Osteoarthritis is chronic; it usually develops as a result of stress on the joint and excessive wear and tear. It can also occur after injury or some other cause of joint inflammation. It may develop because of poor conformation or developmental abnormalities in joints when the animal was young. But often arthritis simply follows years of wear on a joint. In addition, many breeds of dog with long backs, such as dachshunds, are prone to disc disease, while others, such as German shepherds, are prone to hip problems.

There is much that you can do to make a set of steps pet-friendly. Steps are usually 20 cm (8 in) high with 50-cm (20-in) wide treads. If you have a pet, it is best to reduce the height of each step and increase the size of the tread. Where space allows, each step should be large enough to allow your pet to stand on all fours and rest. Perhaps the steps could take a curved or zig-zag route so that they are more gentle. This will make steps much more comfortable for an older pet to use, removing much of the strain on its aged joints and spine.

Building steps from materials that match or are similar to those used in the rest of the garden will help them blend in. If you make

***This flight of steps** is fine for an agile cat, but may be difficult for an older dog with stiffer joints.*

the treads large enough, you will have space for pots and containers. However, you need to think about safety for yourself as well as for your pet. Steps made from tiles or wood can be slippery, making them a hazard for older dogs with weak or stiff limbs. Not only will it be difficult for them to get up the steps, but they are also more likely to fall down them. Textured surfaces that give a good grip, even in poor weather, are preferable. You can use brick or concrete to create the treads, and then infill them with a rougher material such as crushed stone or pea shingle.

Outside access

Even if your dog is a total home lover and would not venture out without you, it is always a wise precaution to put a spring-return on gates and to put up warning signs. Signs let people know that you have a dog, and they will generally close the gate behind them. If they forget, the spring-return will do it for them. 'Please close the gate' sounds polite and suggests that you have a little dog; 'Beware of the dog' is more likely to deter burglars.

While it is important to allow your pets easy access to the garden, it is probably better for visitors and people making deliveries if they can get to your front door without meeting even the friendliest of dogs. Not everyone was brought up with a dog in the family, and many people are apprehensive the first time they meet an unfamiliar dog. There may be no more than a fence or wrought-iron gate between the front garden and the back garden, but it will be much appreciated by nervous visitors.

Gates come in many styles and materials, with prices to suit all pockets. If you want wrought-iron work, try attending an auction of garden statuary or spending some enjoyable days visiting architectural reclamation yards. At the other extreme, if you are seeking something minimalist, a carpenter or blacksmith will probably make one to your design.

No matter what style of gate you choose, there are a few things to consider where pets are concerned. If the gate is too low, an agile dog can easily jump over it. If the gap between the bottom of the gate and the ground is too large or the ground is soft, any adventurous dog can soon dig its way out. For this reason it is best to put a couple of paving slabs or some other hard material in the space between the gateposts. Small puppies and some of the toy breeds are capable of getting through quite narrow gaps and, unless you choose the right gate, you will have to resort to covering the bottom half of it with chicken-wire, at least until the puppy puts on some weight.

Cat- and dog-flaps

A proprietary plastic cat-flap from a pet store is the easiest way to allow your cat access to the garden. Before you cut a hole in your door, it is important to remember that your cat will still be using the flap when it is older and less agile. So, whichever type of cat-flap you choose, make sure that it is set no higher than 6 cm (2.4 in) from the base of the door. This will allow your cat to step rather than jump through it. If you wish to site the cat-flap higher up the door, your cat will undoubtedly be agile enough to launch itself in and out for most of its adult life. However, when its joints stiffen with age, your cat will appreciate being able to slip in and out with as little effort as possible.

Most flaps have locking devices to deter unwanted visitors, and some can be set to allow the cat to enter the house but not leave; useful if you want to confine your cat at night. Remember to lock the cat-flap if you have a female cat that is calling, otherwise you may find that a neighbourhood tom has dropped in and you have a litter of unwanted kittens. Better still, have your cat neutered.

These days, cat-flaps are designed so that they close properly once the cat has passed through, and do not create draughts. Most cats learn to use cat-flaps by themselves, but if your cat has difficulty grasping the idea, you will need to intervene. Start by leaving the cat-flap open for a few days. Make the cat use the cat-flap when it comes home at feeding time by placing its bowl so that the cat can see it from outside. Motivated by food, it should soon get the idea and before long you will be able to release the flap.

Dog-flaps are bigger versions of cat-flaps, and usually come in a range of sizes to accommodate various sizes of dog. If you have one of the toy breeds such as a Yorkshire terrier, Pekinese or toy poodle, the dog-flap will only be slightly bigger than a normal cat-flap and will not require a large hole in your kitchen door. If you are out for part of the day, a dog-flap will allow your dog access to the garden. Elderly people – who might find it irritating or difficult to get out of a comfortable chair to let their little dog in and out – might also find a dog-flap useful. However, if you have a medium-sized breed or a larger one, you are unlikely to want a hole in the door that is nearly as

Little and large. Flaps come in a range of sizes to cater for every cat and dog from a standard-sized tabby (left) to a young Dalmatian (above).

large as the door itself. It is possible to buy dog-flaps that only open when activated by an electronic collar worn by the dog, but these tend to be expensive.

EXERCISE AND SHELTER FOR DOGS

If you are out for part of the day, your dog may be happier left in a secure run in your yard or garden. It can run about in the open while you go about your business, secure in the knowledge that it is safe. The size of the run will be determined by the size of your dog and the amount of time it is likely to spend there: try to be as generous as you can and make the run as large as possible. Even the best-built run will not be a very attractive feature, so it is best concealed in one of the more functional areas of the garden, such as behind the garage. Here, out of sight of the road, your dog is less likely to become involved with passing pedestrians or other dogs and make a nuisance of itself. Make sure the dog has access to shade at all times, and to an adequate supply of fresh water.

A strong wooden framework, covered in a heavy-duty wire mesh, is usually sufficient. Unless the wire is high enough to prevent your dog from jumping out, you will need to cover the run. Likewise, you will need to make sure that your dog cannot dig its way out. Bury the wire well below ground level or construct a brick wall 60–70 cm (2 ft) high round the perimeter and secure the wire to this. If you really want to go to town, construct a run made out of iron railings fixed to a solid plinth, but again ensure that your dog cannot jump out over the top. Ideally the floor of the run should be made from concrete, paving or tarmac and slope to an outside drain. This will make it easy to wash down with a hosepipe, but remember to raise the kennel off the ground, otherwise it will soon rot.

If you want some inspiration and guidance, talk to the staff at your local boarding kennels, as they are likely to have personal experience of building runs themselves or buying professionally-made ones. Either way, if you are a regular client, they are likely to be more than happy to help you. Try to make the run a happy place, where your dog will want to go. Give it toys to play with and reward it with a small treat to get it used to going into the run and being left.

One of the proprietary feeding cubes that have to be rolled around before it will dispense small treats, or bits of complete dried food, will keep a dog entertained for a considerable time.

Cosy kennels

Most dogs live in the house, unless they are working dogs. However, there are benefits in having a kennel in the garden. If you have a safe, secure garden and your dog does not disturb neighbours with its barking, you may want to let it sleep outside in hot weather. If you go out for a couple of hours, you can leave your dog outside, knowing that it has a comfortable place to sleep. Even if you would never dream of leaving your dog 'home alone', a kennel can still become a favourite refuge: cool in the summer and snug and warm on cooler days. Older dogs with stiffer joints and arthritis should not be left out in kennels in cold, wet weather.

There is an ever-increasing range of kennels available in the larger pet stores, made from a range of materials including timber, plastic and fibreglass. These new materials mean that kennels can even be igloo-shaped, and would not look out of place in a modern garden. The size of the kennel is dictated by the size of the dog. It should be large enough for the dog to turn round in comfortably, and sufficiently deep to shelter the dog from rain and wind. A roof that can be removed to enable you to clean out the interior of the kennel is very helpful.

As an alternative to a shop-bought version, you can make a wooden kennel yourself without having to be a skilled carpenter. There are no hard-and-fast rules as to what shape a kennel should be, or what colour it should be finished in, so do not feel obliged to use dull stained timber. With non-toxic wood stains available in a range of colours from the subdued to the exotic, you should soon be able to find a colour that will blend in well with the style of your garden. You could even build a kennel out of brick, breezeblock or stone. If you make a permanent structure that is likely to be in place for a number of years, it is best to incorporate a damp-proof membrane. Your dog will not be grateful for an inhospitable, cold, damp kennel. Neither will you, if it leads to your dog becoming unhealthy.

Lots of pet-friendly features here (opposite)! Raised beds to keep the dog out of the planting, gravel for easy maintenance, and a purpose-built kennel in keeping with the design of the garden.

A dog run allows your dog to exercise in the open air while remaining completely safe. This one is built of wood and heavy-duty wire mesh. Note that the dog has access to shade.

ENCLOSURES FOR CATS

Cats are probably the easiest pet for a city dweller to keep. You can, of course, confine your cat to the house or apartment, but allowing it into the garden will provide it with a much more stimulating life. You need to ensure, though, that the cat cannot get out on to a busy road. Many inner city gardens are part of a terrace, with each small garden separated from adjacent gardens by high walls. A small city garden, surrounded by high wall and secure gates, can simply be covered with chicken-wire or nylon netting, fixed firmly to wooden battens running along the tops of the walls. This will effectively make your garden into a cage: your cat will not be able to get out and neighbourhood cats will not be able to get it. If you choose the wire carefully and let climbers and twiners grow up and over the structure, you will not notice it.

A less radical solution might be to make brackets that project a metre (3 ft) or so into your garden, fix them to the tops of your walls and stretch wire securely between them, so achieving the same effect. The brackets can be metal or wood and should project away from the wall at an angle of 45 degrees. The framework formed by the brackets should be covered with a stiff mesh. The mesh holes should not be bigger than 25 mm (1 in). If the holes are larger, your cat may try to push its head through them and become trapped. It is tempting to use chicken-wire, but as this rots more quickly than other wire mesh, it is probably a false economy. Make sure that all the joins between the sections of wire are secure. This is easily done by leaving generous overlaps between the various pieces of wire mesh, and threading lengths of lightweight wire along the joins. If your cat is a skilled climber, you could add a vertical overhang to the end of each bracket. This should hang down at least 30 cm (12 in) into the garden and be covered with wire mesh in exactly the same way.

You might feel concerned that your garden will look like a cross between a chicken coop and an open prison – but do not despair. You can still let climbers grow up through the wire. Just make sure that there are no woody stems that would allow your cat to climb up and over the barrier. Besides using climbers to soften walls, you can add shelves and ledges for displaying pots, collections of pebbles and shells and, of course, your cats. You will need to make sure that the wall is strong enough to support the weight of shelves and the objects on them. If the wall is sturdy enough you could even take out a few bricks and cement in pieces of slate or paving slab. Position these so that your cat can easily get up to the highest shelf, which will become a favourite basking place and look-out post.

Cat pens

Building a pen for your cat might be a more practical option if your garden is very large, not surrounded by walls, or if you feel you would rather not enclose the entire garden. The pen should look like an aviary, high enough for you to walk around in comfortably, but covered with a larger mesh wire than would be required for birds. You can make the basic timber structure as ornate and complicated as you want, and there is no reason why you should keep to a rectangular shape.

The pen should be as large as possible, and it is unlikely that you will find a suitable structure in a garden centre. You could build it yourself, or have it built to your design. However, you might want to enlist the help of the professionals who supply purpose-built pens and houses for boarding catteries and breeders. You will find their advertisements in most specialist cat magazines.

If you build the pen so that it is adjacent to a wall of your house, you might consider inserting a cat-flap, which will enable your cat to use the pen whenever it likes. The pen should be sited so that it

King of the castle.

A kitten enjoys the view from the top of a wall. Cats like to reach a high vantage point, where they can be safe from danger but react quickly to the sight of potential prey.

receives sun for most of the day. If you provide some old tree-trunks for your cat to climb, and some high vantage points for it to bask on, it will be completely at home.

If you also provide a small cat house that is insulated and draught-free, you may find that your cat is quite happy to use it as a permanent bed and spend the nights there. The cat house should be constructed from a double skin of timber cladding, with a layer of insulating material in the cavity. During frosts your cat will appreciate it if you add some form of heating, such as an overhead infrared light or a heating pad under its bedding.

The floor of the pen can be covered with concrete, pea shingle or bark. If you also add some plants, you can create a little jungle for your urban tiger. Plant grasses, some hardy foliage plants, a few evergreen shrubs, add some seasonal hanging baskets and let climbers find their way up and over part of the structure, and your cat pen will soon blend in with the rest of garden. The usual litter tray, or a small, well-drained pit of sharp sand hidden away in a corner, is all that is needed for a toilet.

Cat pens are particularly useful if you want your cat to breed, if you have an unneutered tom that you do not want indoors, or if your cat is older and no longer alert or fit enough to escape the traffic. You can leave home confident that your cat is totally secure and will be there to greet you when you return. In fact, you and your cat may find the pen so enjoyable that it becomes known as the 'purr-gola'.

'Al-cat-traz': a downtown garden for cats

'Al-cat-traz' is a design option for a smaller urban garden. The designer, Jacquie Gordon, has incorporated interesting features for both humans and cats, and constructed an enclosure within the garden for use when the owner is not there; this is made of wrought-iron sections purchased from a specialist architectural ironmonger. They were chosen to match the style of the house. There is no reason

Cat-Proofing a Tree

Cats are good climbers and think nothing of getting themselves into precarious positions in the tops of trees. Tall trees close to perimeter walls and fences can give your cat an easy escape route, while also allowing other neighbourhood cats an easy way into your garden. Pruning the lower branches may help, but even this is no deterrent to an agile cat.

1. Trim the lower branches up to a height of 2 m (6–7 ft). If the tree is in a designated conservation area, or is subject to a Tree Preservation Order, you should contact the planning department of your local authority before trimming or pruning.

2. Attach a hoop of stiff wire around the trunk just under the lowest remaining branches. Ensure the wire is tight enough to prevent a cat squeezing through, but not so tight that it damages the tree.

3. Put a second loop of stout wire about 1 m (3 ft) in diameter around the tree. Suspend it horizontally from the lowest branches with pieces of wire.

4. Stretch wire mesh between the two loops. Attach it to the lower branches as well, if necessary. The holes in the mesh should be small enough to prevent a cat from getting its head stuck in them. Plastic-coated wire mesh will last longer than chicken wire, and is more attractive.

THE BOTTOMLESS BUCKET

This 'cat-proofing' method is suitable for a slender tree that has a trunk diameter of 30 cm (12 in) or less.

1. Remove the handle from a tall plastic bucket.
2. Use a sharp craft knife to remove the bottom of the bucket. Make a vertical slit up the side.
3. Fit the bucket around the

trunk of the tree about 2 m (6–7 ft) above ground level. If the bucket is too low, the cat may be able to jump above it.
4. Fix the bucket in place with two bands of stout wire. Move the bucket up and down the trunk every year to prevent damage or discoloration to the trunk.

why you could not construct a similar enclosure from wood, but you should ensure that any timber preservative used is non-toxic to pets. Allow treated timber to dry completely before allowing cats to come into contact with it.

There is no need for the enclosure to have a roof, so it is covered with the wire mesh used for the sides. If you want a weather-proof roof, PVC sheeting with an ultraviolet filter is undoubtedly the best solution. This is available from builders' merchants who sell self-build kits for conservatories. Constructing an enclosure with a solid roof is a major task and needs the help of a professional or a competent amateur. You should also check with your local planning department to see whether you need planning permission before erecting such a structure.

To entice the cats into the enclosure all you need do is place their first meal of the day there. If the garden were not secure, the cats would have to be carried to the enclosure. This could prove difficult or tiresome, so it might be better to site an enclosure along a wall of the house. The cats could then come and go through a cat-flap set in a door. If you wish to keep the cats out of the house when you are out, you should choose one of the cat-flaps that allows for variable access, letting the cat into the enclosure, but preventing it from re-entering the house until you return. The entrance to the enclosure should also be secure; make sure that the gate is fastened with a strong security catch, such as a hasp and staple, which can be closed and locked with a padlock.

Within the enclosure the designer has provided a stimulating and practical environment for cats, with cat house and ramp, a tree stump for use as a viewing platform and scratching post, and a sand litter tray and disposal bin. Your cat should be safe and happy within the enclosure and there to greet you on your return. However, two cats will probably be happier than a single cat, so think about getting it a suitable feline companion.

In the main part of the garden, which can be used when you are there to oversee activity, a raised brick-edged pond with gently trickling water provides interest and pleasure for cats and humans alike, while timber viewing platforms placed up the walls provide feline viewing positions.

'Al-cat-traz'

'Al-cat-traz' was designed by Jacquie Gordon, winner of a Gold Medal at her first Chelsea Flower Show in 1999. Jacquie lives in Gloucestershire, England, and shares her small courtyard garden with two cats. This shows the principal pet- and human-friendly features.

Existing eucalyptus with viewing platforms mounted on trunk and netting round base of trunk to prevent too much damage from scratching

Raised timber litter tray filled with sand with adjacent buried disposal bin

Boundary wall with cast-iron ornamental brackets extending out from wall to support mesh frame to prevent cats climbing on to wall

Timber viewing platforms on cast-iron brackets at different heights on wall

Low-level light among planting

Paved terrace for cats to lounge on

Bat-box secured under eaves

Table and chairs for eating on terrace

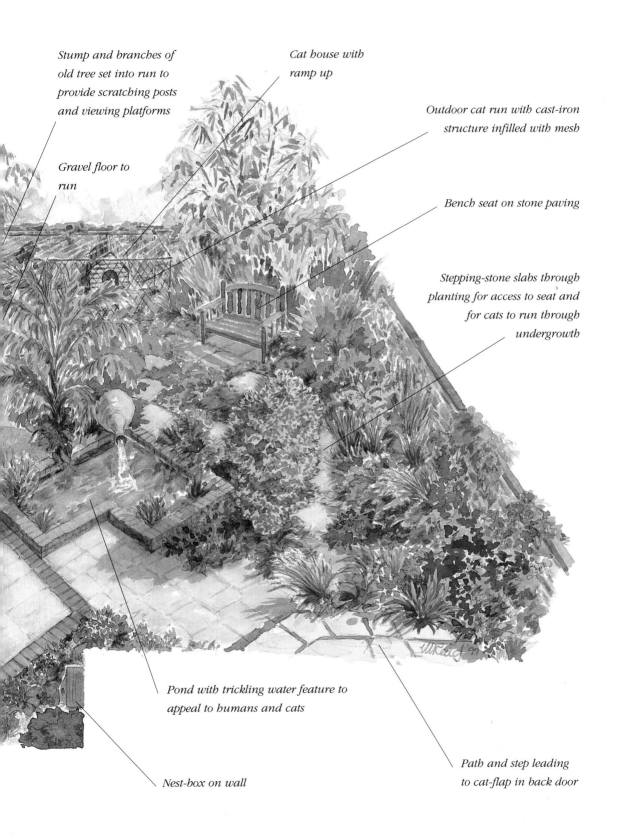

Stump and branches of
old tree set into run to
provide scratching posts
and viewing platforms

Cat house with
ramp up

Outdoor cat run with cast-iron
structure infilled with mesh

Gravel floor to
run

Bench seat on stone paving

Stepping-stone slabs through
planting for access to seat and
for cats to run through
undergrowth

Pond with trickling water feature to
appeal to humans and cats

Path and step leading
to cat-flap in back door

Nest-box on wall

'Al-cat-traz' Design and planting

Wall-mounted mask as focal point

Tree fern as feature

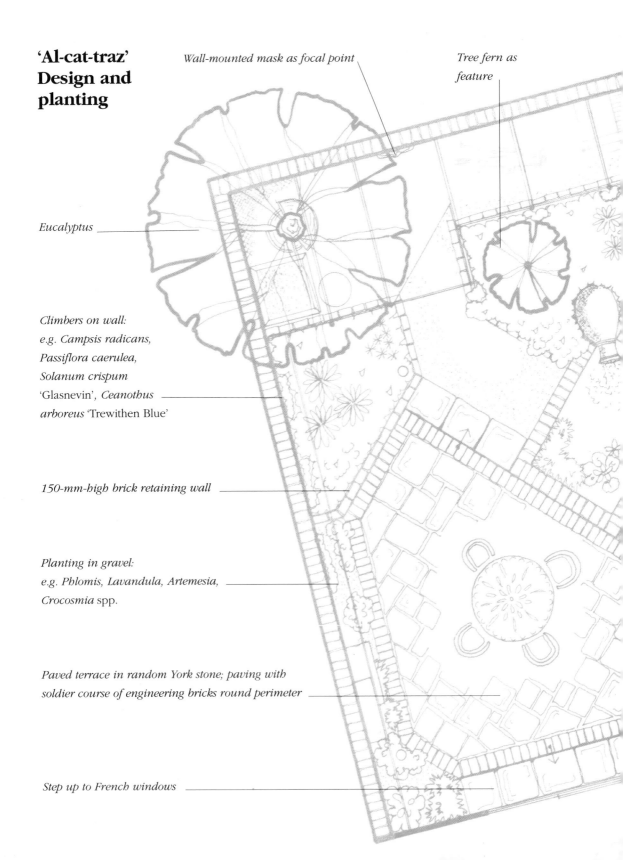

Eucalyptus

Climbers on wall:
e.g. Campsis radicans,
Passiflora caerulea,
Solanum crispum
'Glasnevin', *Ceanothus*
arboreus 'Trewithen Blue'

150-mm-high brick retaining wall

Planting in gravel:
e.g. Phlomis, Lavandula, Artemesia,
Crocosmia spp.

Paved terrace in random York stone; paving with
soldier course of engineering bricks round perimeter

Step up to French windows

Shade tolerant 'jungly' planting behind seat: e.g. *Fargesia murieliae* 'Simba', *Phyllostachys aurea*, *Sasa tsuboiana*, *Acanthus spinosus*, *Hosta fortunei* 'Albopicta', *Helleborus argutifolius/orientalis*

Climbers on boundary walls: e.g. *Eccremocarpus scaber*, *Azara microphylla*, *Jasminum* x *stephanense*

Lush planting around pond: e.g. *Ophiopogon planiscapus* 'Nigrescens', *Pennisetum villosum*, *Bergenia* 'Silberlicht', *Hosta sieboldiana* var. *elegans*, *Molinia caerulea* 'Variegata'

300-mm-high brick retaining wall

Small tree: e.g. *Cornus mas* 'Variegata', *Magnolia* x *loebneri* 'Leonard Messel'

Brick-edged pond, 150 mm above paved terrace but flush with planting at the rear. Tilted urn trickles into pond and perimeter shelves support marginal plants

Existing 2.4-m-high boundary wall

Door with cat-flap

Planting in gravel: e.g. *Cistus, Helianthemum, Agapanthus, Sedum, Sisyrinchium, Osteospermum, Phormium, Incarvillea* spp.

PLANTING LIST FOR 'AL-CAT-TRAZ'

Z=CLIMATE ZONE (see map page 89)

TREES

Cornus mas 'Variegata'
Cornelian cherry with grey-green leaves and creamy white margins **Z6–9**

Magnolia x *loebneri* 'Leonard Messel'
Free-flowering magnolia with magnificent purple-pink flowers **Z5–8**

BAMBOO AND GRASSES

Fargesia murieliae 'Simba'
Compact, medium-sized, shade-loving bamboo **Z6–7**

Molinia caerulea 'Variegata'
Deciduous yellow-green leaves with small purple flowerheads **Z5–9**

Pennisetum villosum
Tuft-forming grass, producing panicles of white bottlebrushes; not reliably hardy **Z8–10**

Phyllostachys aurea
Densely leaved, fishpole bamboo with yellowish-green culms; very tidy and compact **Z6–7**

Sasa tsuboiana
Small bamboo with jungly leaves **Z7–8**

CLIMBERS AND WALL SHRUBS

Azara microphylla
Evergreen shrub or small tree with fragrant yellow flowers; best trained against a warm wall **Z8–10**

Campsis radicans
Trumpet vine, so-called because of its red-orange flowers **Z4–9**

Ceanothus arboreus 'Trewithen Blue'
Fast-growing, evergreen shrub with blue flowers, best against a sunny wall **Z8–10**

Eccremocarpus scaber
Free-growing colourful climber, usually grown as an annual **Z8–10**

Jasminum x *stephanense*
Scrambling climber with fragrant flowers **Z8–10**

Passiflora caerulea
Hardiest of the passion flowers, reknowned for its spectacular flowers **Z8–9**

Solanum crispum 'Glasnevin'
Hardy climber with potato-like purplish-blue flowers **Z7–9**

FERNS

Dicksonia antartica
Most common tree-fern, requiring dappled shade and a sheltered position **Z7–9**

GRAVEL PLANTING

Agapanthus
Perennial with strap-shaped leaves and handsome flowers **Z8–10**

Artemesia
Grey or silverish finely cut leaves **Z4–9**

Cistus
Colourful, semi-evergreen rock rose **Z7–9**

Crocosmia
Orange-flowered herbaceous perennial, also known as montbretia
Z5–9

Helianthemum
Similar to *Cistus* and also confusingly called rock rose
Z7–9

Incarvillea
Perennial with large trumpet-shaped flowers that appear in spring **Z6–8**

Lavandula
Easy to look after, but benefits from a regular trim **Z6–9**

Osteospermum
Low-growing perennial with daisylike flowers **Z9–10**

Phlomis
Jerusalem sage; has woolly grey-green leaves and bright yellow flowers **Z8–11**

Phormium
New Zealand flax; has large strap-like leaves. *Phormium tenax* is the hardiest species
Z8–11

Sedum
Stonecrops come in all shapes and sizes, but all like sun and well-drained soil **Z4–9**

Sisyrinchium
Iris-like leaves with yellow or yellow-blue flowers **Z7–8**

PERENNIALS
Acanthus spinosus
Deeply cut, green leaves topped by purplish, foxglove-like flowers **Z7–10**

Bergenia 'Silberlicht'
Popular, weed-smothering ground cover with white flowers **Z3–8**

Helleborus argutifolius
Evergreen perennial with veined foliage and apple-green flowers in spring **Z7–9**

Helleborus orientalis
Lenten rose, virtually evergreen with softly toned flowers in many shades **Z4–9**

Hosta fortunei 'Albopicta'
Variegated hosta that is more white than green, at least until after flowering
Z3–9

Hosta sieboldiana var. *elegans*
Glaucous-leaved hosta with purple flowers **Z3–9**

Ophiopogon planiscapus 'Nigrescens'
Not really a grass, although commonly called black grass
Z4–9

Building a Bat-Box

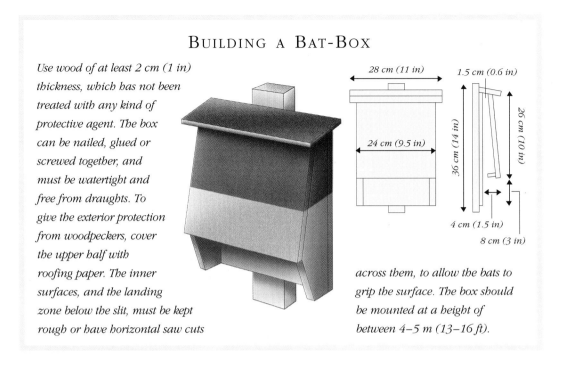

Use wood of at least 2 cm (1 in) thickness, which has not been treated with any kind of protective agent. The box can be nailed, glued or screwed together, and must be watertight and free from draughts. To give the exterior protection from woodpeckers, cover the upper half with roofing paper. The inner surfaces, and the landing zone below the slit, must be kept rough or have horizontal saw cuts

28 cm (11 in)

1.5 cm (0.6 in)

24 cm (9.5 in)

36 cm (14 in)

26 cm (10 in)

4 cm (1.5 in)

8 cm (3 in)

across them, to allow the bats to grip the surface. The box should be mounted at a height of between 4–5 m (13–16 ft).

Cats, bats and birds

Even if you have a cat, you can encourage wildlife to use your garden if you take suitable precautions. If you site a nest-box in the middle of a wall where your cat cannot reach it, members of the tit family will soon make a nest there. Try to choose a wall that receives full sun, because the birds will prefer this. The adult birds are very vigilant and will patiently wait until all signs of danger have disappeared before they visit their nest. When the young are ready to leave the nest, you should confine your cat to the house or to an outside run. The fledglings will drop out of the nest-box and disappear into the undergrowth before they become used to their wings. Obviously, they will be very vulnerable to a cat until they are fully confident fliers.

Cats are much less likely to catch a bat, so you can encourage bats to roost in your garden. You can buy bat-boxes or you can make your own. The more you have in your garden, the greater the chance that bats will occupy them. Bat-boxes need siting at the top of a warm wall, underneath the eaves. If you make your own box, you will need some untreated, thick, rough-cut timber. Assemble the box with brass or galvanized screws rather than wood glue. The entrance should be a narrow slot running along the bottom of the box. The back panel should extend below the entrance and be half sawn through. This will

Rabbit hutches are available in a variety of styles from pet shops, or can be constructed at home from non-toxic wood and paint. Hutches should be as large as possible, and secure from predators.

give the bats a good landing area from where they can crawl up into the safety of the box. If you are lucky, you should soon have some occupants taking to the air on a summer's evening

Shelter and play areas for rabbits

There are no hard-and-fast rules as to what a hutch and run should look like. All rabbits require is a dry, draught-free area for sleeping, a sheltered area so food is kept dry, and as much space for exercise and play as possible. If you do not have the space for a large run, construct a two- or three-storey apartment, connected by well-secured ramps that have horizontal battens so that the rabbits do not slip. They will not only enjoy it, but also benefit from all the exercise.

There is no reason why your rabbit hutch should be dull. Although rabbits will gnaw their hutches occasionally – even if you provide them with pieces of young, non-toxic wood, such as apple and cherry – as long as you use a non-toxic wood dye or preservative, you can stain or paint your hutch in an attractive colour to fit in with the style of the garden.

Think about the location of the hutch when designing your garden. Sunlight is good for

rabbits, as it helps them develop strong bones, but it is not a good idea to leave a hutch against a south-facing wall in the heat of summer. Instead, place the hutch and run where the rabbits have morning or evening sun, and shade during the middle of the day. You should also avoid draughty locations on the side of the house that gets the worst of the wind. If the weather becomes really bad, your rabbits will be happy in their sleeping area, as long as you provide some additional insulation by securing an old piece of carpet or blanket over the hutch.

To prevent the rabbits from escaping or to stop potential predators getting in, a run should have a top and bottom as well as sides. A chicken-wire base is fine for a run on a lawn that allows rabbits to graze, but it is hard on a rabbit's feet and can cause sore, infected hocks. Paving slabs are probably a better solution.

Even a sturdy hutch does not necessarily protect a rabbit from predators. They may be able to bend or break the wire, and agile ones can even open cage doors. The presence of a predator may trigger a panic attack in the rabbit. A rabbit that is running wildly back and forth, or twisting and thrashing about, can easily break its own back, or die from shock. A survivor may be permanently disabled, or develop an infection from a bite or claw wound.

It is, therefore, essential to choose wire that is strong and has no weaknesses, and to make sure that the door to the hutch has a secure fastening. The rabbits' sleeping quarters should be well off the ground so that they are totally out of sight of any potential predator. A large-diameter plastic drainage pipe in the rabbits' run provides a substitute burrow, giving the rabbits somewhere to play and somewhere to hide if they feel threatened.

A portable rabbit run can be moved round areas of fresh grass. A run should have a top and bottom as well as sides, to prevent the rabbit escaping or predators intruding.

Keeping fit

Even two rabbits living together need some mental stimulation. In the wild, rabbits are faced with real-life challenges such as finding food and escaping predators. As pets, with all their food and shelter provided, they can soon become depressed or destructive. Toys and a challenging environment will keep your rabbit interested in its surroundings, particularly if it is a solitary rabbit.

Rabbits also need to be encouraged to exercise to keep them in good shape and prevent them from becoming overweight. Fat rabbits are less able to groom themselves, and this can make them vulnerable to fly-strike in the summer. Provide them with the biggest hutch and

the largest run possible. A pair of bonded rabbits in a good-sized run will chase each other around and make full use of the space. Also, provide things for them to climb on, crawl through, dig into and chew on.

Warrens and adventure playgrounds

A piping warren will provide stimulation and exercise for your rabbit. You can make one using various sizes of plastic or earthenware drainage pipes, available from a builders' merchant, as well as 90-degree corners and junctions to put between the straight sections. You will need to choose pipe with a diameter that allows your rabbit to squeeze through easily. In the wild, the tunnels in warrens are not very wide, but rabbits do not seem to mind brushing against the sides.

You can make your piping warren as large as the run will allow, giving your rabbit a variety of entrances and exits. My children's rabbits even have a chamber in their piping warren. By chance, the entrance hole in the top section of a covered cat-litter tray was just the right size to accommodate the piping. So now they stop off in their chamber, and can frequently be heard thrashing around inside.

A network of pipes lying across a rabbit run will force your rabbits to hop over all the pieces each time they want to get from one end of the run to the other. This will keep them fit and healthy, especially if you place food at the opposite end of the run from the sleeping quarters. However, you do not want your rabbits injured by slipping off a pipe or, worse still, being crushed by a heavy earthenware pipe rolling on them. Loose lengths of straight pipe are the main hazard, as corners and junction pieces generally stay put. So, when you lay out your pipes, make sure that all the pieces are secure. Gluing some straight plastic pieces together and including a few right angles will result in a firm structure. You can stop lengths of plastic pipe from rolling around by gluing two straight pieces together side by side. Unless you attach stabilizers to them, straight pieces of earthenware pipe are best avoided. Before cementing or gluing all the pieces together in a permanent structure, think about cleaning. It might be less difficult or unwieldy to clean if you can take the piping out to hose it down.

If you have space for a larger run, instead of a flat concrete floor, you could make some concrete hills with piping tunnels running through them. As long as the concrete is given a textured finish to prevent your rabbits from slipping in wet weather, it will be the ultimate rabbit adventure playground.

Digging pits

Pet rabbits are, like their wild counterparts, active diggers; they may not need to make themselves a burrow, but the activity is instinctive. In the wild, rabbits scrape at the earth with their front paws to loosen the soil and then use their powerful hindlegs to push the soil out of the way. If the soil is light and easily excavated, they will build an extensive network of passages and chambers with numerous entrances. In places, the tunnels will widen out to allow two rabbits to pass each other, or there will be sharp twists and turns that give the rabbit a chance of escape should a small predator such as a weasel enter the warren.

Rabbits will also dig shallow depressions in open ground, known as 'scrapes'. Sometimes the rabbit will dig a scrape to get access to the roots of grasses and plants in winter, but the main reason for scrapes is thought to be territorial. By clearing away the turf to reveal bare earth, rabbits are creating an obvious sign of their presence that few other rabbits can miss. To be doubly sure, they usually deposit a small pile of droppings on the earth.

If you give them the opportunity, your pet rabbits will try this behaviour on your lawn, leaving you with quite a mess. Even house-rabbits will attempt to dig holes in carpets. Rather than try to stop them from digging, it is better to cater for their needs. Some rabbits are content scraping around in their litter tray, but others will be happier with a digging pit.

Any large container will do, even a child's old plastic sandpit. Half fill it with a mixture of sharp sand and earth, and your rabbit will be in heaven. Try to keep the earth dry, otherwise you will end up with a very dirty rabbit.

Alternatively, you can build your own digging chamber. This should be a strong wooden box that is at least twice as long as the rabbit and wide enough to allow it to turn round comfortably. As you are going to half fill the box with sand and earth, it needs to be fairly deep. A box with a depth of 50 cm (20 in) is probably adequate for the average-sized rabbit. The entrance is best placed high in one side so that, no matter how frantic the digging, most of the earth stays in the box. A lid to exclude most of the light will help to give your rabbit an experience that is as near to the wild as possible, but it should be removable so that you can refresh the earth occasionally. As rabbits are inveterate chewers, all nails and screws should be well hidden. Alternatively use dowel and wood glue to construct the box.

A home for tortoises

Bellis perennis, *the cultivated form of the common daisy, bears attractive flowers and is suitable for planting in a tortoise pit.*

A determined tortoise can climb vertical barriers of a surprising height. To prevent a single tortoise escaping from a tortoise pit, the walls must have a vertical drop of 30–45 cm (12–18 in). The pit can be an excavated area, lined with paving slabs that are securely set at a near vertical angle, or with a wall of construction blocks or bricks. Alternatively, if you do not relish the idea of digging out loads of topsoil, you could make a small timber palisade with vertical sides held in place by corner posts that are sunk into the ground. However, tortoises can burrow, so a pit is a far safer solution. You can use the spare soil to make a mound, or to construct a raised bed.

If you carefully remove any turf before digging your pit, you can use this for lining the floor, allowing the grass and any weeds to

WILD FLOWERS AND WEEDS SUITABLE FOR A TORTOISE PIT

Anthyllis vulneraria Kidney vetch	*Geranium pratense* Meadow cranesbill	*Plantago* Plantain	*Tussilago farfara* Coltsfoot
Bellis perennis Daisy	*Hypochoeris radicata* Cat's-ear	*Polygonum persicaria* Red shank	*Vicia cracca* Tufted vetch
Calestegia sepium Hedge bindweed	*Lathyrus pratensis* Meadow vetchling	*Senecio vulgaris* Common groundsel	*Vicia sativa* Common vetch
Calluna vulgaris Heather	*Lotus corniculatus* Bird's-foot trefoil	*Silene vulgaris* Bladder campion	*Vicia sepium* Bush vetch
Fragaria vesca Wild strawberry	*Malva sylvestris* Common mallow	*Sinapis arvenis* Charlock	*Viola arvensis* Field pansy
Galium odoratum Sweet woodruff	*Medicago lupulina* Black medick	*Taraxacum officinale* Dandelion	*Viola riviniana* Common dog violet
Galium verum Lady's bedstraw	*Myosotis arvensis* Common forget-me-not	*Trifolium pratense* Red clover	*Viola tricolor* Wild pansy
		Trifolium repens White clover	

colonize. There are a large number of common weeds that are safe for a tortoise to eat, and you can scatter their seeds into the pit. The list on page 57 excludes any that have airborne seeds that may invade other areas of the garden.

DEMARCATION LINES WITHIN THE GARDEN

Dogs and cats will generally keep off areas of dense planting, so the sooner you can establish some evergreen ground cover underneath your shrubs and between your perennials, the more successful you will be. If you leave patches of bare earth while waiting for bulbs or annuals to appear, cats and dogs will be attracted to the beds.

A few words of reinforcement while your dog is still a puppy will soon teach it where the no-go areas are, but you need to put some thought into where these areas should be first. If you position a flowerbed directly between the kitchen door and the back gate, do not be surprised if your dog runs straight through it when their favourite member of the family appears. Instead, map out the main routes that your pets are likely to use in getting around the garden. They will probably want to get to and from exactly the same places as you do – from the garage to the kitchen door and from the front gate to the front door. If you have not already established paths that take obvious routes between such points, it is a good idea to redesign the main routes around the garden, before your dog makes alternatives for you.

Establishing ground cover and allowing smaller plants to reach maturity can take a few seasons, and there is much that you can do to help them on their way. In addition to feeding them in their growing period, plant some thorny deterrents such as *Berberis darwinii* in strategic spots where your dog would normally venture into a bed. After a few years, when the rest of the planting has established itself, you can transplant these deterrent plants to another area of the garden or, if you feel they have already earned their keep, you can simply dispose of them.

Eye-level barriers are another method of deterring dogs from areas of planting. Again, these can be temporary structures until the planting reaches maturity and can take care of itself, or

Eye-level barriers,
such as this rope strung between wooden posts, is surprisingly effective at keeping a dog out of flowerbeds.

Box hedging is the perfect barrier to deter a dog from going into the planting in this formal garden.

they can be made permanent features. Rope strung between wooden posts at your dog's eye level is both attractive and effective, but there are many other possibilities.

Edging beds with low-level box hedging will deter pets from wandering into planting. Box hedges are a traditional feature in many formal gardens, and are easy to maintain, requiring little more than an annual feed and trim. Even if you have a large area to edge, this solution can be very cheap if you plan ahead, invest in some good stock plants and propagate your own bushes. A single bush will provide a huge number of cuttings that will root directly in the soil. This will take quite a long time, however.

Because the vegetable garden has expanses of bare soil during the spring while you are waiting for seedlings to appear, it will be attractive to cats and dogs. The fine tilth you have created in which to sow your seeds will be appealing to any cat looking for a toilet. Covering the seeds with an array of twigs or fine brush might work as protection for them. A dog that has not been taught that soil is a no-go area will see bare soil as a great place to dig. If possible, it may be preferable to partition off the vegetable patch with a fence and a gate to keep your dog out.

A garden that is all on one level always seems to be missing something, so a few raised beds may be the solution. They allow you to grow plants that need special growing conditions, such as lime-haters in an area of alkaline soil. They also create small microclimates around them. On their shady side you can plant low-growing perennials that do not like full sun. Plants preferring warmer conditions will thrive on the sunnier side.

In a garden with dogs, raised beds really come into their own as the ultimate deterrent. If the bed is constructed so that it is slightly higher than the dog's eye level, you will be surprised at how little

Raising a bed is
another way of keeping
a dog off planting. In
this low bed, treated
timber between low posts
is strong enough to
support the bed.

interest is shown in the planting above. There is a wide range of materials to choose from to construct a raised bed. Your choice will probably depend on your budget and the overall style of the garden. Engineering bricks and facing bricks are suitable for outside use, and will blend in with a more formal urban garden. Natural or reconstituted stone will look better in a country garden. Brick or stone will require strong foundations, and you may need to seek the help of an expert bricklayer, especially if you want to create curved beds. Heavy-gauge timber such as railway sleepers will give a more contemporary feel.

If you want a cheaper solution, you could try timber posts. Using these, you can create beds of almost any shape quite easily. The posts need to be well buried, otherwise the weight of the soil will lead to your bed collapsing. You should only use timber that has been pressure-treated with a preservative, otherwise it will rot off below the ground and your raised bed will come tumbling down. Preserved or pressure-treated timber is usually slightly green. If you do not like

CONSTRUCTING A RAISED BED

The most popular materials for building a raised bed are dry stone, brick and railway sleepers. With all methods of construction, ensure proper drainage for the soil either by leaving gaps in the brickwork or between the sleepers, or by installing drainage tubes. The retaining wall should ideally be about 18 in (45 cm) high. However, if a brick wall is to retain a large and high bed, build a concrete foundation at least 16 in (40 cm) deep, and angle the wall with a backward slope of 1:12.

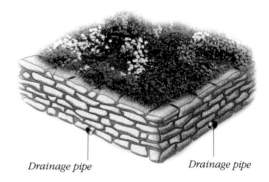

Drainage pipe   *Drainage pipe*

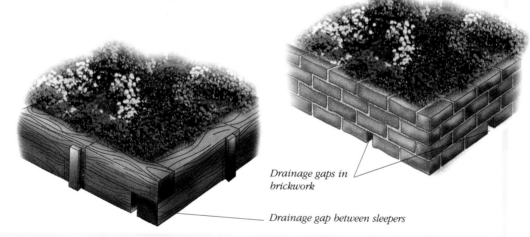

Drainage gaps in brickwork

Drainage gap between sleepers

this, you can paint the posts with a timber preservative. These come in a whole range of shades. Lining your bed with a butyl liner or heavy-duty polythene sheeting will help give the timber a longer life. Just line the back of the posts to keep the soil off them, fixing the lining with an industrial stapler. If you want to create a bed for growing plants that like damper soils, you could line the entire bed. However, unless you want to create a bog garden, you should puncture the lining to provide some drainage.

TOILET ARRANGEMENTS

When designing your garden, you will have to accept that – if you have pets – they will use your garden as a toilet. You can train dogs to use certain areas only, though, and even cats can be encouraged to use a specific area and discouraged from digging up seeds.

Dog loos

No matter how frequently you walk your dog, it will at some time pass faeces in your garden. These should be picked up as soon as possible. All dogs can get worms and these can be passed to humans, making them ill. Very rarely, these worms can infect a child's eye so badly that it may have to be removed. Common sense and scrupulous hygiene are essential at all times, particularly if children are around.

Sniffing and circling are often signs that a dog wants to relieve itself. Ideally it should be trained to use an area of long grass away from the house and from areas used by children.

Collecting faeces is not a pleasant task. If it is frosty, they freeze hard, smell less and can be scooped up on a shovel. Generally, however, the most hygienic method is to place a polythene bag over the hand like a glove, grab the offending article and then pull the bag over your hand by grasping the open neck with two fingers. Make it airtight as quickly as possible, either with a bag tie or by tying an overhand knot, and drop it into the household waste bin.

You can buy dog loos, which can be sunk into the ground in a spare part of the garden. If biological chemicals are added regularly, the waste completely degrades and the dog loo never fills up. They might appear expensive but, aside from a small expenditure on chemicals, they require no maintenance and will last for many years. If you site them under a large shrub or a tree, you have the added benefit that your dog's waste is being turned into a readily available fertilizer for what is probably a very greedy feeder.

A DOG WASTE-DISPOSAL SYSTEM

Dog toilets are designed to break down dog waste and eliminate odours. The plastic tank is sunk into the ground and surrounded by stones. A harmless bacterium digests the waste and reduces it to a safe liquid form, which is absorbed by the surrounding soil.

Stones or rubble

Plastic tank with overflow holes

Digested waste material can be flushed out into earth around

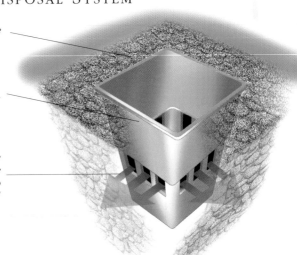

A bitch passing urine on a lawn will discolour it, so teach your pet to use a specific part of the garden, such as an area of longer grass well away from the house. This is not as difficult as it may sound, particularly if you start with a young puppy. After feeding, when it wakes, when it has not urinated for some time, or whenever it shows of wanting to do so, accompany your dog into the garden and encourage it to follow you to the spot you want it to use. When it has done its business, reward it with praise and a treat and it will soon get the idea. Before long, it will automatically return to the spot of its own accord.

If you are out for much of the day, you will probably need to train your new puppy to relieve itself on newspaper. Once the puppy has got accustomed to using a small area of paper, you can gradually move the paper nearer to the door. On a clear day, place the paper outside and leave the door open. Eventually, you can do away with the paper altogether and concentrate on getting your puppy to use the part of the garden you would prefer. If your garden is small and there is no particular place for your dog to defecate, it is better to get rid of any lawn and provide an expanse of shingle. Your dog will be quite happy to use this and it can easily be washed down every few days with a safe disinfectant.

Outside cat-litter trays

Gardeners tend to worry about cats digging into their flowerbeds and scratching up seedlings. Deterrents advertised range from chemicals to high technology sonic scarers, undetectable to the human ear but guaranteed to send any cat scurrying away. Try some of these devices by all means, but there are better ways to tackle the problem.

Cats are very clean animals and are rarely difficult to toilet train in the house. As long as the litter tray is in a quiet place and the litter is fresh, little training is needed. The same applies out in the garden. Cats will seek out the best-prepared piece of ground they can find. They will revel in being able to shovel the soil out easily, and will secretly be thanking you for putting so much effort into cultivating your plot. The answer from a gardener's perspective is to keep bare earth to a minimum. Ground cover is one option, as long as you do not plant *Nepeta* (cat mint), as that will entice all the neighbourhood cats into your garden. If it fits in with the style of your garden, you could try mulching with shingle. Even the most muscular tom cat is likely to think twice about heaving gravel around to do its business.

The vegetable plot, where there is bound to be wide expanses of soil – at least until the new crops appear – is always going to be the most difficult part of the garden. As far as the cat is concerned, the ideal toilet is something that is clean, well-drained and easy to dig in. If your vegetable patch fits these criteria, then unfortunately the cat will tend to use that, so it is a good idea to provide a better alternative in the hope that it might leave your seedlings intact. Try covering newly worked areas with fine brush or twigs so that cats cannot dig out your seeds. Planting upturned clear bottles full of water seems to scare cats away. No one quite knows why, although it is thought that when they see their exaggerated reflection through the glass, they think it is another cat and run off.

Cats love sharp sand. It fulfils all their requirements: it is easy for them to dig in, drains better than any soil and does not mess up their coats. So why not provide them with a pit of sharp sand or children's play sand over a base of rubble or gravel to make it free-draining? Sift it now and again to remove any waste. If you camouflage the pit with grasses, no one will ever know that it is there, and the cat will be even happier having some privacy. This is a perfect solution for a garden of any size. If there are young children around, you should create the cat toilet in a raised bed to keep it safely out of their way. If the children have a sandpit of their own, you should always keep it covered when they are not using it, otherwise cats will happily use that as a toilet instead.

Rabbit droppings can be used a fertilizer for greedy plants. Simply scatter it as a mulch beneath hardy shrubs and bamboo (opposite), or make it into a liquid feed for applying on other crops such as tomatoes (above).

Organic rabbit waste

While waste from dogs and cats can cause disease and must be disposed of hygienically, rabbit droppings are useful in the garden. Rabbits are herbivores, and will live happily on a diet of grass or hay, supplemented with an occasional piece of root vegetable. This is what they would eat in the wild and, as long as they also have access to water, it is all that they actually need. Their unique digestive system

evolved to suit a high-fibre, low-protein and low-energy diet; giving them anything else can lead to health problems.

To get the maximum goodness from what is essentially a poor-quality diet, the rabbit has evolved a special method of digestion called caecotropy. You may have seen a rabbit apparently eating its droppings. There is no reason to be disgusted or alarmed. The rabbit is eating caecotropes (partially digested particles of fermenting food sealed in a coating of colic mucus), which provide more nutrients for the rabbit when they are ingested again. It is a brilliant piece of evolution.

Rabbits are naturally clean animals and, in the wild, use latrine areas well away from their burrows. Being prey animals, they do not want to show a potential predator where their warren is. In a confined space such as a hutch, rabbits will choose a distinct spot to deposit their urine and most of their droppings. Consequently, getting them to use a litter tray is usually very simple. You put a litter tray where they choose to go and most rabbits get the idea straight away. This makes it much easier to keep a hutch clean, but is no excuse for not being fastidious in washing it down with a proprietary disinfectant once a week.

Some rabbits like to kick litter out of their tray. You can get covered litter trays, designed for cats, that the rabbit may accept. However, it might equate the covered tray with its warren and refuse to use it. A litter tray with higher sides may be a better solution. Litter should be non-toxic, dust-free and absorbent. However, it should not form large clumps when damp. Rabbits frequently eat their litter, so it is important that it contains no toxins and that it will not swell up inside their stomach, as many of the clay-based cat litters would. It is, therefore, better to use an organic litter.

As long as you do not apply too much in any single place, you can empty your rabbit litter and droppings directly on to the garden as a mulch, compost it, or use it in a wormery along with other waste vegetable matter, such as peelings. Rabbit droppings are about the only pet waste that can be safely used in this way. Dry rabbit waste contains 2.7 per cent nitrogen, 1.5 per cent phosphoric acid and 1 per

'Suburban Seclusion'

The original 'pet-friendly' show garden was designed for the Blue Cross animal welfare charity and PetPlan by Clare Palgrave, and exhibited at Hampton Court Palace flower show in 1997. This garden has been designed for a busy family with a medium-sized dog and a cat. The garden is a modest size, measuring just 8 m x 8 m (26 ft x 26 ft). The materials are readily available from any garden centre or hardware store, and many of the features are well within the capabilities of an amateur home-improvement enthusiast.

Jungly planting for cats

Long grass for cat digestion

Tiered and shady sitting shelves

Wickerwork tunnel for play and shade

Scratching posts

Herringbone brick paviours for easy cleaning

Seating for humans

Brick for basking

Raised toilet for cat

Arbour =
boundary for
dogs, and
shade for
humans

Dog kennel
beneath tree
providing shelter
and shade

Raised pool for
dog, and
fountain for cat;
water sights and
sounds for
humans

Posts with eye-level rope to deter
pets from planted areas

'Suburban Seclusion'
Design and planting

Shrubs including *Amelanchier lamarckii,*
Nandina domestica, Kerria japonica,
Elaeagnus x *ebbingei, Cornus alba*
'Elegantissima'

Perennials edging arbour, e.g.
Geranium x *magnificum,*
Geranium macrorrhizum 'Album',
Alchemilla mollis

Planting round the circular patio
includes *Catalpa bignonioides*
'Aurea', *Artemesia arborescens,*
Salvia officinalis 'Icterina', *and*
Pennisetum alopecuroides

Stipa gigantea

Scabiosa caucasica
'Clive Greaves'

The gravel path is edged with e.g.
Origanum vulgare 'Aureum' *and*
Sisyrinchium striatum 'Aunt May'

Wall, 60-cm high
retaining mound of
soil to give plants height

Arbour

Milium effusum
'Aureum', *Tolmiea*
menziesii 'Taff's
Gold'

Sea-smoothed
shingle

Patio with table
and chairs

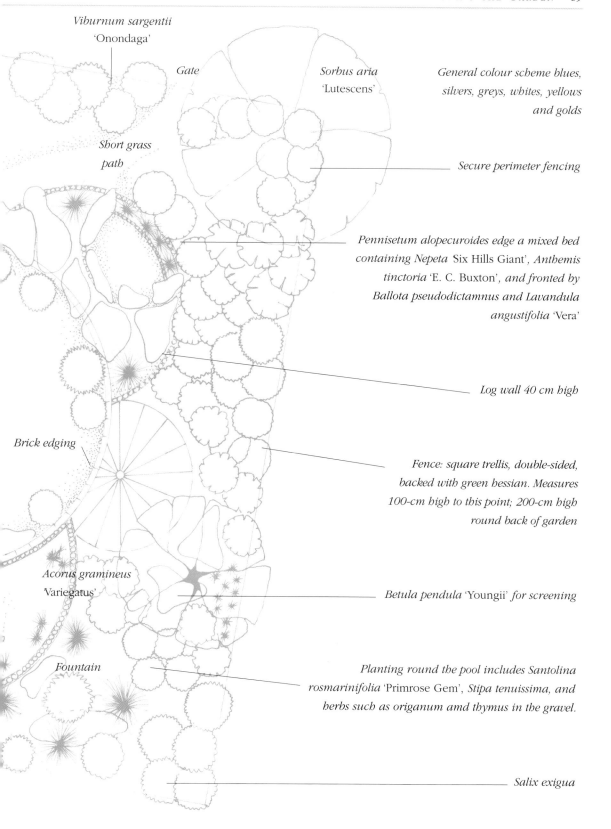

Viburnum sargentii
'Onondaga'

Gate

Sorbus aria
'Lutescens'

General colour scheme blues,
silvers, greys, whites, yellows
and golds

Short grass
path

Secure perimeter fencing

Pennisetum alopecuroides edge a mixed bed
containing Nepeta 'Six Hills Giant', Anthemis
tinctoria 'E. C. Buxton', and fronted by
Ballota pseudodictamnus and Lavandula
angustifolia 'Vera'

Log wall 40 cm high

Brick edging

Fence: square trellis, double-sided,
backed with green hessian. Measures
100-cm high to this point; 200-cm high
round back of garden

Acorus gramineus
'Variegatus'

Betula pendula 'Youngii' for screening

Fountain

Planting round the pool includes Santolina
rosmarinifolia 'Primrose Gem', Stipa tenuissima, and
herbs such as origanum amd thymus in the gravel.

Salix exigua

PLANTING LIST FOR 'SUBURBAN SECLUSION'

TREES

Acer negundo 'Variegatum'
Variegated box elder with green
and white leaves **Z3–9**

Betula pendula 'Youngii'
Silver birch that is dome-shaped
when mature **Z2–5**

Catalpa bignonioides 'Aurea'
Large golden heart-shaped
leaves and long bean-shaped
seedpods **Z7–9**

Sorbus aria 'Lutescens'
Silver-grey whitebeam **Z5–7**

SHRUBS

Amelanchier lamarckii
Spring-flowering shrub with
good autumn colour. Can be
grown as a tree **Z5–7**

Artemesia abrotanum
Aromatic, threadlike soft green
leaves **Z5–8**

Artemesia arborescens
Evergreen, silver-white feathery
leaves, slightly tender **Z5–8**

Ballota pseudodictamnus
Small sun-loving shrub with
grey-green leaves **Z5–9**

Buddleia alternifolia
Arching shrub with silvery
leaves and fragrant lilac flowers
Z5–9

Cornus alba 'Elegantissima'
Red-barked dogwood with
variegated leaves **Z3–8**

Elaeagnus x *ebbingei*
Dark evergreen leaves with
silver undersides **Z6–9**

Euonymus alatus
Winged spindle, oval leaves
that turn dark red in autumn,
and corky growths on stems
Z4–9

Euonymus europaeus
'Red Cascade'
Deciduous shrub colouring red
in autumn **Z4–8**

Kerria japonica
Small-leaved deciduous shrub,
green stems in winter and
yellow flowers in spring **Z5–9**

Lavandula angustifolia 'Vera'
Pale lavender flowers **Z6–9**

Leycesteria formosa
Deciduous, heart-shaped leaves
and red cascading flowers **Z7–9**

Nandina domestica
Heavenly bamboo, evergreen
and upright with good winter
colour **Z7–9**

Salix exigua
Shrubby willow with fine
silvery leaves; good in sandy
soils **Z6–8**

Sambucus nigra 'Albovariegata'
Variegated elder **Z5–7**

Sambucus racemosa 'Plumosa
Aurea'
Red-berried elder with finely
cut golden leaves **Z3–6**

Santolina rosmarinifolia
'Primrose Gem'
Small evergreen shrub with fine
green foliage and pale yellow
flowers **Z6–9**

Viburnum opulus 'Aureum'
Golden guelder rose **Z3–8**

Viburnum 'Pragense'
Evergreen with deeply wrinkled
leaves **Z5–8**

Viburnum sargentii 'Onondaga'
Maple-like leaves, bronze-red
in spring and autumn **Z6–7**

PERENNIALS

Alchemilla mollis
Lady's mantle, good for ground
cover **Z4–8**

Anthemis tinctoria
'E. C. Buxton'
Ox-eye chamomile with lemon
yellow flower **Z4–8**

Artemesia 'Powis Castle'
Woody perennial with feathery
silver leaves **Z7–9**

Geranium macrorrhizum
'Album'
Semi-evergreen, hardy
geranium with white flowers.
Good for dry shade **Z4–8**

Geranium x *magnificum*
Vigorous, clump-forming,
geranium with violet-blue
flowers **Z4–8**

Melissa officinalis 'Aurea'
Lemon balm with gold leaves
Z4–9

Mentha x *gracilis* 'Variegata'
Ginger mint with gold-flecked
leaves **Z5–9**

Nepeta 'Six Hills Giant'
Catmint with very large leaves
Z6–9

Origanum vulgare 'Aureum'
Golden-leaved wild marjoram
Z4–8

Salvia officinalis 'Icterina'
Golden sage **Z5–9**

Scabiosa caucasica 'Clive
Greaves'
Lavender-blue scabious **Z4–9**

Sisyrinchium striatum
'Aunt May'
Variegated, sword-shaped
leaves with pale yellow flowers
Z7–8

Tanacetum parthenium
'Aureum'
Golden-leaved feverfew **Z8–9**

Tolmiea menziesii 'Taff's Gold'
Golden 'piggyback plant',
excellent for shade **Z6–9**

GRASSES

Deschampsia cespitosa
Evergreen tufted hair grass with
airy flowerheads **Z4–9**

Helictotrichon sempervirens
Evergreen perennial grass with
grey-blue leaves **Z4–9**

Milium effusum 'Aureum'
Bowles golden grass, semi-
evergreen and self-seeding.
Cats like to chew it **Z5–8**

Pennisetum alopecuroides
Evergreen Chinese fountain
grass with purple bristles
Z5–10

Stipa gigantea
Semi-evergreen, golden oats
Z5–10

Stipa tenuissima
Perennial grass with feathery
panicles. Even looks good
when dead **Z7–10**

POND PLANTS

Acorus gramineus 'Variegatus'
Evergreen, variegated swordlike
leaves **Z4–10**

cent potash. It is also highly concentrated: 64 kg (141 lb) of rabbit manure is reported to contain the same nutritional equivalent as 100 kg (220 lb) of horse manure. In some countries you can buy fertilizer made from dried, concentrated rabbit droppings. To have a self-sustaining supply to cater for the average garden, you would need a considerable number of rabbits.

If you like liquid feeds, collect 3 kg (6½ lb) of droppings in a hessian bag and hang it in the water butt for a few days, stirring occasionally. Throw the used droppings out as mulch. The liquid becomes a high-quality feed that is suitable for tomatoes and other greedy feeders.

My children's rabbits have quite a special relationship with the garden. I use their droppings to mulch my collection of hardy bamboos. These are gross feeders, and their annual growth is more or less proportional to the amount of fertilizer they get. They thrive on the rabbit droppings, and I frequently have to thin out any old or weak culms. The rabbits devour the culms' leaves and tender growth, leaving only the thicker woody sections. If that is not self-sustaining, organic gardening, what is?

WATER, PONDS AND POOLS

Other than the Turkish Van, few breeds of cat willingly take to water. Many breeds of dog, however, have an instinctive urge to swim – no matter how cold it might be. Retrievers, spaniels, Newfoundlands and poodles are renowned swimmers. Take them for a walk along a riverbank or a beach and, if you let them, they will be thrashing about in the water at the first opportunity. It is natural for dogs to swim, so you might as well let them do so if they enjoy it. The mobility of dogs with skeletal or arthritic conditions is often much improved if they are allowed to exercise in water. Aquatherapy, or hydrotherapy, is increasingly recommended by veterinary surgeons as physiotherapy for such cases.

Garden water features are very appealing to most humans; however, water features of any kind, especially swimming

It is almost impossible to keep some breeds of dog such as this Gordon setter out of water.

pools and ponds, can present a hazard for all pets. On a hot day, a dog with a fondness for water is likely to take over the garden pond with a complete disregard for fish and water plants, let alone the plastic liner, which can easily be completely ruined. If you have electricity powering a fountain or underwater lighting and have not installed a circuit breaker, the dog could be electrocuted. Outdoor and indoor swimming pools, training pools, hot tubs and Jacuzzis can be equally dangerous. It is not unknown for a puppy or an old or infirm dog to fall into a pool, expend all its energy trying to get out, and drown before it is discovered. I have even heard of a horse having to be winched out of a swimming pool. After breaking into a garden and rushing across the lawn, it failed to notice the difference between the grass and the green pool cover.

Dogs can easily drown if they fall into an outdoor pool and there is no one around to help them out. Keep unattended pets away from pools, or ensure they have a means of climbing out without difficulty.

Not all animals are as lucky as that horse. Tragedies do happen, particularly at night when the family is asleep. Keep pets well away from pools when there is no one on hand to keep an eye on them. Lock internal and external doors to keep dogs away from swimming pools during the hours of darkness. Design your swimming pool so that it is as pet-proof as possible. This may mean having raised walls on all sides except one. This end should have a shallow area to enable any pet that has inadvertently fallen in to walk out easily. Hedgehogs are also prone to falling into open pools during the night. Although they are surprisingly strong swimmers, they will drown unless they can get out. A short plank of wood left floating on the water gives hedgehogs something to climb on to and rest on until they are rescued.

Outside taps

No gardener likes having to traipse into the house to fetch water or to connect a hose to the mains. Having a water tap installed on an outside wall costs very little and, as long as you have an internal stopcock installed so that you can drain down external pipes to prevent them bursting in hard frosts, it will be trouble-free. If you live in the country and have an active dog, you will save the cost of installing that tap many times over. How many times have you been out walking on a wet day and had your dog push past you into the hall, shaking itself all over the walls and leaving a procession of muddy paw-marks on the carpet?

The easiest answer is to give your dog a gentle hose-down from that external tap. Naturally your dog will not relish the prospect, and you will have to take a firm hold of its collar with one hand, while playing the hose over its belly and lower legs with the other. But in no time at all you will have a clean dog. Let it into the kitchen, give it a rub down with a towel, followed by a treat, and it will soon forgive you.

If you place the tap so that water runs into a nearby drain or soaks away into an area of pea shingle, it will save you the trouble of having to brush it away. The cost of having a plumber install the outside tap will probably be offset by your long-term savings on cleaning fluids and decorating materials.

Ponds for dogs

Before you build any water feature in a garden, you should consider what you want in it and what you want to keep out of it. If your dog is one of the breeds that has a natural love of water, it will be happy to plunge into water on a hot summer day. Northern breeds, such as the husky and the malamute, may be prevented from excavating large holes to cool themselves if they have a pool available. All dogs seek out shade to cope with hot weather, but many will enjoy having their own plunge pool as well.

Ideally, a plunge pool for a dog should be constructed from reinforced concrete, and painted with a black waterproof sealant. Such a pool will last for years, but it is a major undertaking. Not only will you need to dig a sizeable hole, you will also need large amounts of concrete, as the walls of the pool should be at least 10 cm (4 in) thick. But it may well prove its worth, especially if you have one of the larger breeds. You can even construct a ramp at one end so that your dog can walk in and out easily. The end result may look like a glorified sheep-dip, but with some creative landscaping, such as a bold piece of sculpture next to it, or water cascading into it from a spout, you can make a dramatic feature that blends in with the rest of the garden.

One of the most stunning plunge pools I have seen was constructed for a family spaniel in a small courtyard garden. It was a small, circular pool made of reinforced concrete, which was shallow round the edge, so that the dog could get in and out easily, but also deep enough to cover the dog to the shoulder. In the centre, a single spout of water cascaded from a pipe hidden in an old, weathered

Keeping water plants to a minimum means there is nothing for a dog to get tangled up in if it decides to take a dip. Keeping a pool shallow gives a pet a safe and easy exit. In the interests of safety, you should always use a low-voltage pump.

stone pillar. The pump and the electric cable were contained in the plinth supporting the pillar, so the dog could not come to any harm.

Fibreglass or plastic is a cheaper and easier alternative to concrete, but if your dog is going to swim you will need to get the deepest and strongest liner you can find. Check that the moulding is reinforced and that it is the thickest gauge available. Butyl liners are more than adequate, but always use the heaviest grade you can find. It may be expensive, but it is less likely to get punctured by your dog's claws. As an additional safeguard, consider lining the bottom of the pond with paddlestones. These are flat stones that have been smoothed over a long period of time by the action of water. Your local aquatic centre should have a supply, so there is no need to remove them from a natural environment.

Whether you build a dedicated plunge pool or create a garden pond with modifications so that your dog can dip in it now and again, it is advisable not to be too fussy with planting. Stick to the big and bold. Your dog will not get tangled in vegetation and your pond will look the better for it. To prevent accidents, stick to low-voltage pumps for fountains and waterspouts, and always use a circuit-breaker. Features such as fountains should always be separate from the area where the dog might bathe, and power cabling and water pipes should be well concealed beneath a layer of stones.

If you would like a pond, but do not want your dog to take dips in it, apply some of the same principles used to keep pets off flowerbeds. Construct eye-level deterrents such as low walls made of brick, stone or timber, and plant the pond so densely that there is little water to be seen.

Water features for cats

Cats have very efficient kidneys that enable them to survive on a small amount of water. However, they should have access to a supply of clean water at all times. Some cats seem to drink very little in their owner's presence, but can be found lapping up a puddle somewhere in the garden. Do not worry; as long as the water is reasonably clean, your cat will come to no harm. If you notice that your cat is drinking excessively, it may be a sign that it has some underlying illness and you should consult your veterinary surgeon as soon as possible.

Decorative, trickling water features will fascinate your cat. As long as the water is reasonably fresh, your cat can safely use it for the occasional drink while out in the garden. Unless they are water-loving breeds such as the Japanese bobtail or Turkish Van, cats prefer to keep away from large expanses of water. Most cats will enjoy brimming pools that bubble gently, or pools that overflow into a lower reservoir. Both types can be kept small and are well suited to urban gardens. Unless you want to stock them with masses of aquatic plants, they need not be particularly deep, and the bottom can be disguised with stones.

Some cats are expert at catching fish in garden ponds, especially if there are

Rivulets of water spill *from copper spouts in this terracotta water feature designed to appeal to cats. The trickles are gentle enough for cats to play in, and also provide a soothing background noise for humans.*

CREATING A CAT-FRIENDLY WATER FEATURE

The construction of this water feature is very simple and uses readily available materials.

What you will need

• *Four terracotta pots of varying sizes. Make sure that they have sufficient overhang at the rim to enable the copper spouts to be attached*
• *One x 2-m (6.6-ft) length of 15-mm ($^1/_2$-inch) diameter hosepipe*
• *One x 1-m (3.3-ft) length of wider diameter hosepipe (wide enough to fit over the 15-mm ($^1/_2$-inch) diameter pipe)*
• *Low-voltage pump with an adjustable flow.*
• *Smooth paddlestones (obtainable from garden or aquatic centres)*
• *One 15-mm ($^1/_2$-inch) jubilee clip*
• *Readimix concrete*
• *Tube of flexible sealer*
• *Copper sheet*

How to construct the fountain

1. Feed the 15-mm diameter hosepipe through the bottom of pot D. Make sure it protrudes at least 30 cm (1 ft) above the top of the pot.
2. Feed the wider hose over the smaller one until it reaches the bottom of pot D.
3. Mix a small amount of concrete and fill pot D to within 10–13 cm (4–5 in) of the rim.
4. Trim the wider diameter hose level with the top of the concrete.
5. Thread the top section of the smaller hose through the hole in the base of pot C.
6. Push pot C into the concrete to create a stable base for it, but remove the pot once the concrete starts to set.
7. Once the concrete is set, reposition pot C in the concrete and trim off the excess hose to

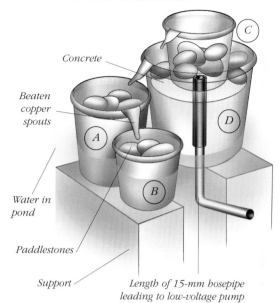

Concrete

Beaten copper spouts

Water in pond

Paddlestones

Support

Length of 15-mm hosepipe leading to low-voltage pump

leave a 5 cm (2 in) protruding into pot C. A jubilee clip can be attached round the hose to secure the pot.
8. Fill the holes in the remaining pots with flexible sealer.
9. Cut the copper sheet into triangles. Shape these into spouts to hang on the pots. If you have difficulty, a blacksmith might help.
10. Build the support in the pond (blue engineering bricks or frostproof building blocks would be good choices). Construct your fountain, using stones to hide the support and any exposed hose.
11. Connect the pump according to the manufacturer's instructions and experiment with various levels of flow. You may need to adjust the spouts a little at this stage.
12. The fountain should not require much maintenance, but remove the pots from the pond during winter to prevent frost damage.

shallows where the fish can get stranded. If your cat, or one of the neighbourhood cats, is skilled at fishing, you have problems. The cat will not change its behaviour, no matter what you do. Short of getting rid of the cat or the fish, the only solution is to make the pool cat-proof. The easiest method is to design a pool where the minimum depth of water at any point is no less than 25 cm (10 in). If you want a formal, regularly shaped pool, adding a retaining wall with a top that is 25 cm (10 in) or more above the level of the water is a further deterrent. With the water so far below the level of the top of the wall, the cat is usually unwilling to risk tumbling in when it tries to swipe at a passing fish. As long as the water is not too deep and the cat can leap out, a ducking will do it no harm and will teach it to leave your pond alone. If all else fails, install a noisy, voluminous fountain or waterspout, which should scare unwanted cats away.

Planning for older pets

Improvements in animal health care over the last few years have increased the life expectancy of our pets. Better diets, vaccinations against deadly or debilitating diseases and constantly improving veterinary care have meant that more pets reach old age. Cats now routinely live into their teens and occasionally into their twenties, and some dogs, particularly the smaller breeds, live well into their teens. Like humans, pets do not suddenly become geriatrics. Old age creeps up on them. This stage of their lives can last nearly as long as their adult stage and, if we plan for it, can be just as fulfilling as their younger years. By this age, our pets really are part of the family, totally loyal, and still able to give us much enjoyment.

Older dogs can find it difficult to cope with smooth surfaces such as tiling. If they are arthritic or have weak leg muscles, they may struggle to get up and could easily slip and lose their balance. They will have difficulty getting up and down steps and will appreciate help. Ramp access to the lawn (as in the large country garden design, pages 80–85) will not only help the dog; it also makes life easier for the gardener when using a wheelbarrow.

You should also be prepared for changes in your pet's character and behaviour as it grows older. It is likely to become more lethargic, easily confused and to sleep for longer periods. It may also become less tolerant and short-tempered. Bear this in mind when older pets come into contact with other people, particularly children. It is sensible to keep an aged and fretful dog confined in the back

***Sleeping for long periods** is one of the effects of old age in a pet. Simple measures can be taken around the garden to enable older pets to enjoy their later years.*

garden so visitors can come and go without the risk of aggression.

Check your cat's access routes into the garden to see if you can make things easier for it. If you are happy for your cat to wander, but it is having difficulty scaling the back fence, consider putting easy steps up it or even inserting a cat-flap.

Clip back thorny hedges and look out for barbed wire and stray nails. Ponds and swimming pools are a great hazard to elderly dogs. If they fall in and are too weak to climb out, they will exhaust themselves in their panic and drown. This is not uncommon, so fence off ponds and pools and make sure that your dog can not get near them, especially at night.

The Rural Idyll

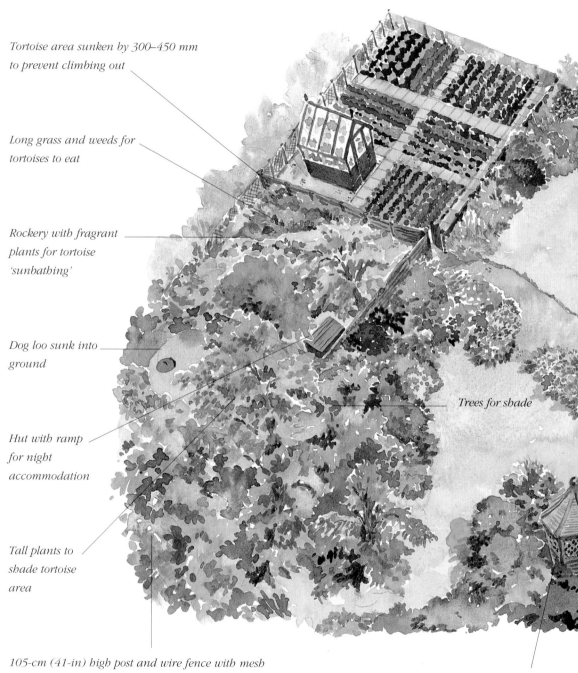

Tortoise area sunken by 300–450 mm
to prevent climbing out

Long grass and weeds for
tortoises to eat

Rockery with fragrant
plants for tortoise
'sunbathing'

Dog loo sunk into
ground

Hut with ramp
for night
accommodation

Tall plants to
shade tortoise
area

Trees for shade

105-cm (41-in) high post and wire fence with mesh
buried 30 cm (12 in) into ground and turned outwards
to prevent burrowing by wild rabbits

Gazebo with semi-circular
paved terrace in front

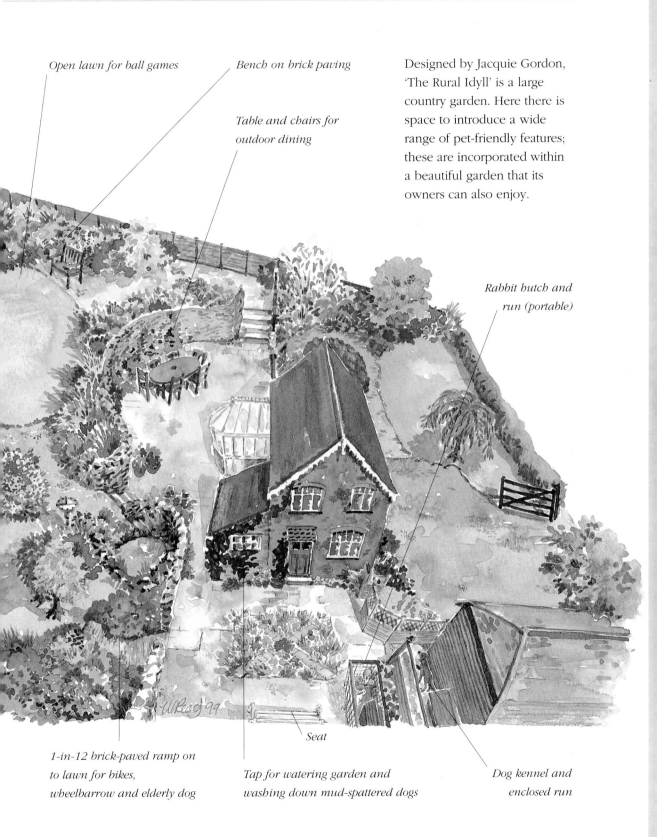

Open lawn for ball games

Bench on brick paving

Table and chairs for outdoor dining

Designed by Jacquie Gordon, 'The Rural Idyll' is a large country garden. Here there is space to introduce a wide range of pet-friendly features; these are incorporated within a beautiful garden that its owners can also enjoy.

Rabbit hutch and run (portable)

Seat

1-in-12 brick-paved ramp on to lawn for bikes, wheelbarrow and elderly dog

Tap for watering garden and washing down mud-spattered dogs

Dog kennel and enclosed run

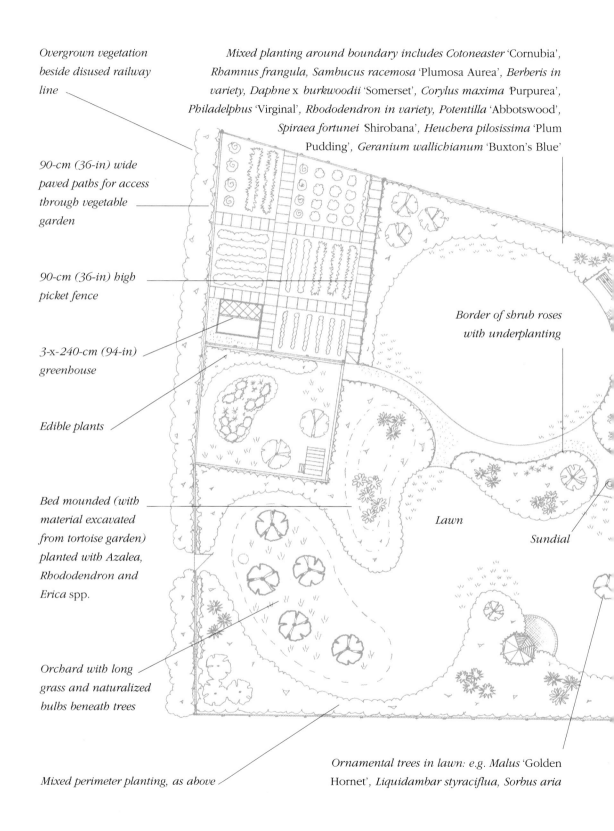

Overgrown vegetation beside disused railway line

Mixed planting around boundary includes Cotoneaster 'Cornubia', Rhamnus frangula, Sambucus racemosa 'Plumosa Aurea', Berberis in variety, Daphne x burkwoodii 'Somerset', Corylus maxima 'Purpurea', Philadelphus 'Virginal', Rhododendron in variety, Potentilla 'Abbotswood', Spiraea fortunei 'Shirobana', Heuchera pilosissima 'Plum Pudding', Geranium wallichianum 'Buxton's Blue'

90-cm (36-in) wide paved paths for access through vegetable garden

90-cm (36-in) high picket fence

Border of shrub roses with underplanting

3-x-240-cm (94-in) greenhouse

Edible plants

Bed mounded (with material excavated from tortoise garden) planted with Azalea, Rhododendron and Erica spp.

Lawn

Sundial

Orchard with long grass and naturalized bulbs beneath trees

Mixed perimeter planting, as above

Ornamental trees in lawn: e.g. Malus 'Golden Hornet', Liquidambar styraciflua, Sorbus aria

75-cm (30-in) high stone wall round terrace with scented planting through gravel around perimeter, e.g. Phlomis italica, Lavandula spica, Caryopteris x clandonensis 'Worcester Gold'

75-cm (30-in) high wall with 105-cm (41-in) trellis on top with matching gate

'The Rural Idyll'
Design and planting

Gravel garden with planting of ornamental grasses, bamboo, hostas, ferns: e.g. Miscanthus sinensis 'Zebrinus', Ophiopogon planiscapus 'Nigrescens', Festuca glauca, Hakonechloa macra 'Aureola', Fargesia murieliae 'Simba', Phyllostachys aurea, Hosta tardiana 'Halcyon', Hosta sieboldiana var. elegans, Hosta fortunei 'Albomarginata', Matteuccia struthiopteris, Athyrium nipponicum 'Pictum'

Mixed boundary hedge

Front lawn

Steps up   Conservatory

Herringbone brick path

Ornamental planting

Gravel forecourt

Double gates

Back door   Gate

108-cm (43-in) high trellis

Pond with waterfall set into bank with e.g. Astilbe, Primula, Hosta spp. and Houttuynia cordata 'Chameleon'

Herb garden with paved paths through

Garage converted from small barn

PLANTING LIST FOR 'THE RURAL IDYLL'

TREES

Liquidambar styraciflua
Sweet gum, grown for its
brilliant autumnal colour **Z5–7**

Malus 'Golden Hornet'
Small tree with a profusion of
golden crab apples in autumn
Z5–7

Sorbus aria
A small spreading whitebeam
with silver-grey foliage, white
flowers and brown-red fruit
Z5–7

BAMBOO AND GRASSES

Fargesia murieliae 'Simba'
Medium-height, shade-loving
bamboo **Z6–7**

Festuca glauca
Sun-loving blue grass **Z5–6**

Hakonechloa macra 'Aureola'
Low mound-forming grass with
yellow variegated leaves **Z5–6**

Miscanthus sinensis
'Cosmopolitan'
Variegated grass capable of
reaching 2.5 m (8 ft) **Z7–8**

Miscanthus sinensis 'Zebrinus'
Large grass with striking yellow
bands across the leaf **Z7–8**

Phyllostachys aurea
Densely leaved, fishpole
bamboo with yellowish green
culms, very tidy and compact.
Z6–7

FERNS

Athyrium nipponicum
'Pictum'
Low spreading fern with dark
red stems and silvery, metallic
fronds **Z3–8**

Dryopteris wallichiana
Evergreen fern with near-black
stems **Z4–8**

Matteuccia struthiopteris
The spectacular ostrich fern is
happiest in rich moist soils
Z2–8

Phyllitis scolopendrium
Evergreen fern with long green
fronds **Z4–8**

Polystichum setiferum
'Proliferum'
Soft shield fern with deeply
cleft fronds arching from a stout
central crown **Z5–8**

HEATHERS

Erica carnea
Long-lasting winter heath, many
new varieties are tolerant of
alkaline soils **Z5–7**

PERENNIALS

Astilbe
Deeply cut foliage and plumes
of pink flowers, prefers moist
soils **Z4–8**

Geranium wallichianum
'Buxton's B lue'
Dense, deep-green foliage with
long-lasting, lavender-blue
flowers **Z4–8**

Heuchera pilosissima
'Plum Pudding'
Neat evergreen foliage with
dark red flowers **Z4–8**

Hosta fortunei 'Albomarginata'
Early-flowering hosta with
white margins around the
leaves **Z3–9**

Hosta tardiana 'Halcyon'
Glaucous blue foliage with
mauve flowers **Z3–9**

Hosta sieboldiana var. *elegans*
Similar to 'Halcyon' with leaves
up to 50 cm (20 in) across
Z3–9

Houttuynia cordata
'Chameleon'
Rapidly spreading, brightly
variegated leaves and scented
flowers **Z5–9**

Lavandula spica
Old English lavender **Z6–9**

Ophiopogon planiscapus
'Nigrescens'
Highly fashionable, but not
really a grass **Z6–8**

Primula x *bullesiana*
Candelabra primula in a range
of colours **Z5–8**

SHRUBS
Berberis spp.
Easy going, adaptable
barberries that thrive in most
soils **Z4–9**

Caryopteris x *clandonensis*
'Worcester Gold'
Attractive shrub with green-
gold leaves that contrast with
the bright blue flowers **Z6–9**

Corylus maxima 'Purpurea'
Purple filbert, best pruned each
winter **Z5–8**

Cotoneaster 'Cornubia'
A vigorous shrub with bright
scarlet fruit **Z7–8**

Daphne x *burkwoodii*
'Somerset'
Semi-evergreen shrub with
fragrant pink-blushed flowers
Z5–9

Philadelphus 'Virginal'
Hybrid 'mock orange' with
strongly scented white flowers
Z5–8

Potentilla 'Abbotswood'
Long-flowering shrubby
cinquefoil with a profusion of
white blooms **Z3–8**

Rhamnus frangula
Evergreen buckthorn needing a
warm position **Z9–10**

Rhododendron spp.
A genus covering the dwarf
Japanese azaleas and the large
Himalayan rhododendrons
Z7–9

Rosa spp.
Choose disease-resistant
varieties if possible **Z5–9**

Sambucus racemosa
'Plumosa aurea'
Ornamental elder with yellow,
finely-cut foliage **Z3–6**

Spiraea fortunei 'Shirobana'
Dense, rounded bush that
carries both white and red
flowers on the same plant
Z4–8

Planting the garden

T he key to planting a successful garden is planning and research. Filling your trolley at the garden centre with plants that appeal to you on the spur of the moment is usually a recipe for disaster. You can find many excellent plant books that are crammed with useful information for less than the price of a couple of shrubs. If they help you to choose the right plants for your soil, your aspect and the style you are trying to achieve, it will be money well spent.

If you are to have a pet-friendly garden that looks as good as the one opposite, it will need careful planning.

Although your pet will influence your choice of plants, your garden has to satisfy your needs as well. You will want to make it a haven for relaxing and entertaining. You will probably also want it to reflect a certain style. This may mean continuing the look and feel you have already achieved inside the house. You will also want the garden to look good throughout the year, and you will need to plan for this. Successful planting is about manipulating different sizes, shapes and colours of plants, foliage and flowers to achieve a satisfying look overall.

Although a well-planted garden may look like the work of an artist, if you follow the steps below you will find that successful gardening is more of a science than an art, and is acheivable by anyone who takes the time and trouble to select plants that suit their particular garden.

SOIL TYPE

If you want a problem-free garden that is easy to maintain, you must establish whether your soil is acid or alkaline. If it is heavily alkaline, there are certain plants, such as azaleas and pieris, that will not thrive in your garden unless you are prepared to grow them in containers, or to construct raised beds and routinely feed the plants with ericaceous fertilizer. If the soil in your garden is heavily acidic, plants such as rhododendrons, azaleas and other lime-haters will thrive, but there are other species that it may be best to avoid. It is dangerous to

assume that all the plants sold in your local garden centre will thrive in your garden. Gardens that are just a short distance apart can have totally different soil. It is always advisable to test your soil with a soil-testing kit and to use a good plant guide to identify plants that will grow well in your garden and those that should be avoided.

CLIMATE AND MICROCLIMATES

Find out the maximum and minimum temperatures for your area. Then, unless you are prepared to make a special effort, or you have some warm south-facing walls in your garden, limit yourself to plants that will survive the hardest winters. Your regional meteorological office should be able to provide this information for you.

The plants listed in this section are all referenced according to the hardiness zone system that was developed by the United States Department of Agriculture. This system records the average annual minimum temperature for each zone. Each plant is then allocated a zone range that represents the lowest temperatures it should be able to survive without damage. The plant may, of course, be grown in any zones warmer than those specified. There may also be smaller microclimates – such as well-drained sunny hillsides – where plants allocated to warmer zones will grow quite contentedly. On the other hand, some plants that are indicated as hardy in your zone may fail to thrive due to your garden's particular aspect. A plant's survival is more unpredictable at the extremes of each zone.

Every garden has a number of microclimates. Some parts will be in full sun all day, while others will be in permanent shade. A wind-free area against a south-facing wall will get the benefit of summer sun, and you will be able to grow more tender plants there. But an exposed bed that gets little sun needs hardier plants that will tolerate such conditions. Always remember the golden rule that 'plants do not grow where we want them to; they grow where they can.'

STYLE AND DESIGN

When you have assessed your soil and climate, you can start to list plants that will fit in with the style you are trying to achieve. Do not be disappointed if you end up with a limited list of plants. Gardens that keep to a small number of species often look far better than those that have been based on a 'pick-and-mix' approach. You might also want to restrict yourself to a limited palette such as silver and grey or gold and yellow.

The hardiness zone system, developed by the US Department of Agriculture, is a guide to the average annual minimum temperatures experienced in each zone. The plants listed in this book have been given a zone range within which they should be able to grow successfully. Plants can also be grown in warmer zones than those allocated. The zone system is not foolproof, however, and local microclimates should be taken into account as well.

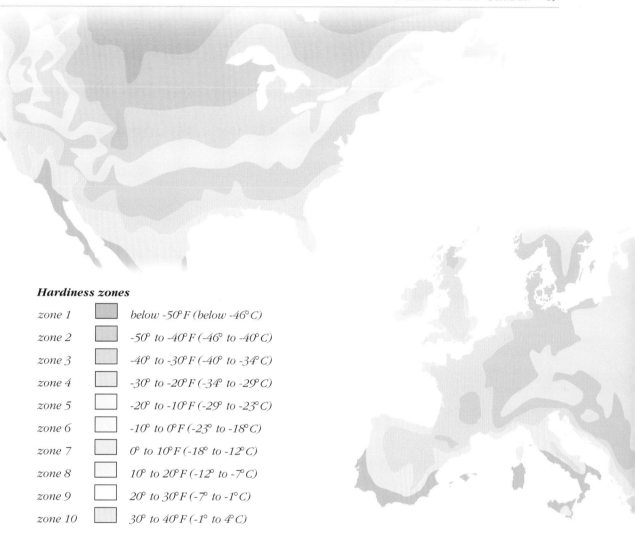

Hardiness zones

zone		temperature
zone 1		*below -50° F (below -46° C)*
zone 2		*-50° to -40° F (-46° to -40° C)*
zone 3		*-40° to -30° F (-40° to -34° C)*
zone 4		*-30° to -20° F (-34° to -29° C)*
zone 5		*-20° to -10° F (-29° to -23° C)*
zone 6		*-10° to 0° F (-23° to -18° C)*
zone 7		*0° to 10° F (-18° to -12° C)*
zone 8		*10° to 20° F (-12° to -7° C)*
zone 9		*20° to 30° F (-7° to -1° C)*
zone 10		*30° to 40° F (-1° to 4° C)*

Key plants and skeleton plants

No matter how small your garden, you should ensure that you have some key plants that establish the main visual link between the garden and the surrounding buildings or landscape. This might be a single tree as a focal point at the end of a view, or an exotic specimen that dominates the main planting. If you have a large garden, each part of it might have a key plant that sets the tone and feel for that area.

Skeleton planting provides the basic bones of the garden. It is usually evergreen and gives year-round interest. It may include screening plants or climbers to fill a blank wall or to hide monstrosities such as the oil storage tank. Evergreen shrubs tend to take a number of years to reach maturity, so you should always try to visualize the garden as it will look in five years' time rather than

Evergreen shrubs

provide the structure for
seasonal infill such as
perennial grasses,
angelica and geranium.

next year. In the meantime, plant annual climbers or fast-growing hardy climbers until the evergreen achieves its full, mature size.

Unless you have a particularly large garden, you should remember that plants are generally not viewed in isolation. There is usually something behind them, such as the garage wall, the neighbour's house or a view. The style and planting of the garden should complement this view rather than conflict with it. Your structural planting of trees and shrubs can help provide the link between your garden and its surroundings. So, no matter whether you are planning a modern, minimalist garden or a more traditional country garden, take great care in selecting and placing these key plants. They are the bones on which the rest of the garden hangs.

Colourful infill

These are the plants that will complement your structural planting and bring colour to the garden through the seasons. Start with the bigger shrubs and work down to the smaller perennials. Limit yourself to large drifts of the same species, rather than using too many single plants. Finally, add in seasonal bulbs and annuals.

THE IMPORTANCE OF SEASONAL INTEREST

Undoubtedly the most successful gardens are those that provide interest throughout the year. Aside from architectural plants grown for their stunning foliage, few plants are at their best all year. Most give a stunning display of flowers for a few weeks before fading. A few, such as spiraea, flower in spring and go on to have wonderful tinted foliage in the autumn. To achieve interest throughout the year, plants should be grouped so that, between them, they always provide a good display of flowers or foliage. This means considering the characteristics of each plant – its flowering period, foliage, potential size and extent, and whether it has interesting berries or bark during the winter. The best way to guarantee interest across the seasons is to plan each part of the garden, producing a calendar of what plants will be at their peak in each month and making sure that each bed and each view has something to delight the eye.

However, too much variety can make your garden too busy. Big, bold planting that is based around a limited number of species will look much more effective, and is certainly the best way to start a new garden. If, after one year, you find the garden too bleak, you can always add some different varieties. By then you will know which parts of your garden need improving at a certain time of the year. If you start by planting too many species, you may find that you cannot make yourself uproot unsuitable plants that are already happily established, and so end up by compromising the overall design of your garden.

Once the big plants are placed, work down towards the smaller species, paying particular attention to colours and textures. Do not forget the smaller evergreens such as lavender, santolina, senecio, hebe, cistus and salvia. It is surprising how much colour can be introduced into a garden through foliage rather than flowers. An added benefit of this type of planting is that many of these plants can grow in drier conditions and will withstand drought better.

PET-FRIENDLY PLANTING

Dense planting throughout the year will look attractive and have the added benefit of keeping dogs and cats off beds. Extensive patches of bare earth waiting for this year's annuals or perennials to appear will be an instant attraction to animals, who will quickly start to dig. This does not mean that annuals and perennials cannot be incorporated into the overall scheme, but that you should make sure there is a sufficient number of evergreen species to provide interest throughout the year. Conifers may seem like the obvious choice, but they can be very dull. There is a huge range of other evergreen shrubs and trees available, many with a wide variety of leaf colour and texture. Some evergreens flower

Dense planting of *shrubs and perennials along this grass path gives year-round interest and helps to keep dogs and cats off beds.*

during the year, although their flowers tend to be less showy than those of deciduous plants.

Pet-resistant plant stems

When planning your pet-friendly planting, choose species that are robust enough to cope with being trampled on, rather than delicate plants that probably need to be confined to containers until they are large enough to survive. Anything with brittle branches should be avoided or sited well out of the way. From the moment I first saw one in full bloom, I wanted to have a sizeable oak-leafed hydrangea (*Hydrangea querquifolia*) in my garden. Not only does it give a wonderful display of white mop-heads in summer, there is the added bonus of leaves that turn red and purple in the autumn. However, the weight of the flowers and its brittle branches mean that as soon as a dog brushes past, the plant usually loses a branch. After three years, it is no bigger than the day it arrived from the nursery.

When you have active pets, the solution is multi-stemmed plants that are pliable enough to snap back when they are bent over. Willows and bamboos are perfect examples. Whereas an elegant shrub supported on a single unbending stem usually becomes a casualty, a multi-stemmed plant only has to regrow a missing branch.

Keeping planting dense on corners and island beds will deter a dog from taking short cuts. Spiky plants, such as this hardy palm, will also act as a deterrent.

Strategic planting

On island beds and corners, where a dog is likely to take shortcuts, planting should be particularly dense, leaving no obvious gaps for it to squeeze through. Once a dog starts to make a route across a bed, it may be difficult to stop it. Instead, it is easier to prevent the situations from arising in the first place. A few prickly plants such as berberis or holly will act as a deterrent until other planting becomes mature enough to form a complete barrier.

Pests and disease

Some plants are almost impossible to grow successfully without using pesticides and chemical controls. Because pets and garden chemicals are not happy bedfellows, it is advisable in a pet-friendly garden to stick to disease- and pest-resistant plants. There enough plants to choose from without lumbering yourself with a speciality that will never look good unless you resort to the horticultural equivalent of advanced chemical warfare.

Plant interest for pets

Grasses and plants with large leaves not only give interest throughout the year but provide a natural jungle for cats. Younger cats will play with the drooping seedheads, while older cats will lurk happily in the cover waiting for unsuspecting prey to appear. Cats like their own secret thoroughfares; if you leave a bit of space between the boundary fence and the plants at the back of the border, they will use this tunnel to get round the garden.

Many modern perennial planting schemes incorporate grasses. This makes an interesting habitat for a cat. One of the leading exponents of this new type of perennial planting is Piet Oudolf. About 20 per cent of the planting in his garden at Hummelo in the Netherlands consists of hardy grasses, which become a dominant feature in the autumn and winter once the perennials have died back. In the US, leading designers Wolfgang Oehme and James van Sweden are following a similar path in seeking to bring the vanishing landscape of the prairie into their gardens. Combining drifts of grasses such as *Calamagrostis acutiflora* and *Carex morrowii* with largely native perennials such as eupatorium and rudbeckia, they create gardens that require little maintenance, have few pest problems and are totally pet-friendly.

The same desire to create low-maintenance gardens using native plants led to the tussock gardens of Australia and New Zealand. Plants such as cortaderia and chionochloa are interspersed with a host of sedges (carex) and larger plants such as cordyline and phormium. These plants are all hardy and robust, well capable of being buffeted by gales or a charging dog. Planted in gravel, the tussocks and grasses create a perfect jungle for the antipodean cat.

Cats like their own jungles for stalking and hunting; long grasses and overhanging planting such as this willow provide ideal conditions.

VERTICAL PLANTING

Climbers are invaluable, particularly in smaller gardens where they offer an extra dimension without taking up scarce ground space. They are equally useful in larger gardens, where they can be used to disguise ugly necessities or to soften large expanses of wall and fence. Wall shrubs or climbers on a house soften the transition between the verticals of the building and the horizontals of the garden.

Climbers can also be used to cover a pergola. This can provide a shady retreat for a pet in a garden that is in full sun for most of the day. Dogs will move between sun and shade to regulate their body temperature. If there are no naturally shady areas in the garden, a pergola may be the ideal solution: your dog is more likely to use the garden, and to stay with you when you are out enjoying the sun.

Some climbers such as ivy and climbing hydrangea have hairy, suckerlike aerial roots and are self-supporting. Although they may be slow to become established, eventually they need no other support and will extend over their allotted space. As long as your wall is sound, there is little danger of plants such as ivy damaging your house. Other climbers, such as clematis and sweet pea, have tendrils, and will need a support such as trellis or wire to twist and twine round. Other than making sure that the support is strong enough to support the climber when it is fully grown, there are no hard-and-fast rules. You can even allow climbers, such as clematis, to scramble through other plants. By choosing a climber and a host plant that come into bloom at different times of the year, you can maximize the amount of colour in the garden.

VERTICAL PLANTING

Acacia dealbata
Silver wattle, mimosa
Self-supporting **Z8–10**

Actinidia chinensis
Chinese gooseberry
Needs support **Z8–9**

Akebia quinata
Chocolate vine
Needs support **Z5–9**

Campsis radicans
Trumpet vine
Needs support **Z4–9**

Ceanothus spp. (most)
Californian lilac
Wall shrub **Z8–10**

Chaenomeles speciosa
Japonica
Needs support **Z5–9**

Clematis spp.
Clematis
Needs support **Z5–9**

Cotoneaster horizontalis
Fishbone cotoneaster
Self-supporting **Z5–8**

Cytisus battandieri
Moroccan broom
Self-supporting **Z7–8**

Eccremocarpus scaber
Chilean glory vine
Needs support **Z9–10**

Garrya elliptica
Silk-tassel bush
Self-supporting **Z8–10**

Humulus lupulus
Common hop
Needs support **Z6–9**

Hydrangea anomola
subsp. *petiolaris*
Climbing hydrangea
Self-supporting **Z4–8**

Itea ilicifolia
Sweetspire
Self-supporting **Z8–10**

Lonicera spp.
Honeysuckle
Needs support **Z5–9**

Magnolia grandiflora
'Exmouth'
Magnolia
Self-supporting **Z7–9**

Parthenocissus tricuspidata
Boston ivy
Self-supporting **Z4–8**

Passiflora caerulea
Common or blue
passion flower
Needs support **Z8–9**

Polygonum baldschuanicum
Mile-a-minute or
Russian vine
Needs support **Z5–9**

Vitis coignetiae
Crimson glory vine
Needs support **Z5–9**

Wisteria sinensis
Chinese wisteria
Needs support **Z5–9**

Clematis macropetala
(*opposite left*) *is a
popular climber that
needs the support
of a trellis.*

*A **pergola** can help
create an area of shade
that will be a relief for
both dogs and humans
in warm weather.*

In addition to the true climbers, there are shrubs, such as cotoneaster, ceanothus and fremontodendron, that will thrive against a wall. They may need tying to a support and regular pruning but, as long as the soil at the foot of the wall is not allowed to become dry and impoverished, they will thrive. The wall should also create a warmer microclimate that will help you to grow more tender shrubs.

SHADE-LOVING PLANTS

Even if you have a large garden that is not overlooked by a neighbouring property, you will still have areas of shade. Your

The contrasting foliage of a blue-leaved hosta and the golden feverfew brings interest to a shady corner.

boundary walls and fences will create areas of shade and, as soon as you start planting trees and larger shrubs, you will make others. Some areas will be permanently in shade, while others will only be in shade for part of the day. Areas beneath trees may be in dappled shade.

Shade comes in two forms: dry shade beneath large trees and damp shade in the shadow of buildings. If you choose plants that are suited to these conditions, shade is rarely a problem. As long as you identify the shady parts of your garden and choose plants that tolerate such conditions, they should grow successfully. However, a large tree will take all the nutrients from the soil around it, leaving little but dry dust. Although there are plants that can tolerate such conditions, your plants will do much better if you dig in plenty of compost and manure before planting and then mulch the area with a good layer of compost each spring.

Because they have to survive with less light, shade-loving plants tend to have large, attractive leaves. This means that shady areas can be made very lush and junglelike. Their flowers may be insignificant

SHADE-LOVING PLANTS

Alchemilla mollis
Lady's mantle
Moist **Z4–8**

*Amelanchier
lamarckii*
Serviceberry
Dry **Z5–9**

Anemone x *hybrida*
Moist **Z4–8**

Aruncus spp.
Goat's beard
Moist **Z4–8**

Astilbe spp.
Moist **Z4–8**

Aucuba japonica
Spotted laurel
Any **Z7–11**

Bergenia spp.
Dry **Z3–8**

Betula pendula
Silver birch
Dry **Z4–8**

Brunnera spp.
Any **Z4–8**

Buxus sempervirens
Common box
Dry **Z5–9**

Camellia spp.
Moist **Z7–9**

Danäe racemosa
Alexandrian laurel
Dry **Z7–9**

Eleagnus x *ebbingei*
Dry **Z7–10**

Epimedium alpinum
Barrenwort
Dry **Z4–9**

Fargesia spp.
Bamboo
Moist **Z7–9**

x *Fatshedera lizei*
Any **Z8–11**

*Ferns (Asplenium,
Polypodium,
Polystichum)*
Dry **Z4–8**

*Ferns (Blechnum,
Matteuccia,
Osmunda)*
Moist **Z2–8**

Hypericum x
inodorum 'Elstead'
Dry **Z6–8**

Lamium spp.
Deadnettle
Dry **Z4–8**

Ligustrum spp.
Privet
Moist **Z5–11**

Liriope muscari
Lilyturf
Dry **Z6–10**

Lonicera pileata
Honeysuckle
Dry **Z5–9**

Luzula spp.
Woodrush
Dry **Z5–9**

Omphalodes spp.
Moist **Z6–9**

Osmanthus spp.
Dry **Z7–9**

Pachysandra
Moist **Z4–8**

Polygonum spp.
Knotweed
Moist **Z3–9**

Pulmonaria spp.
Lungwort
Dry **Z4–8**

Ribes sanguineum
Flowering currant
Dry **Z3–8**

Ruscus aculeatus
Butcher's broom
Dry **Z7–8**

Sambucus racemosa
Red-berried elder
Dry **Z3–6**

Sarcococca spp.
Sweet box
Moist **Z6–8**

Skimmia spp.
Any **Z7–9**

Symphoricarpos albus
Snowberry
Dry **Z5–7**

Symphytum spp.
Comfrey
Dry **Z5–9**

Tellima grandiflora
'Purpurea'
Fringecups
Dry **Z4–9**

Tiarella cordifolia
Foamflower
Dry **Z3–8**

Tolmiea menziesii
Piggyback plant
Dry **Z6–9**

*Viburnum
rhytidophyllum*
Any **Z6–8**

and softly coloured, but many are fragrant and will bring an extra dimension to the garden.

Some of the leathery-leaved evergreens such as fatsia and camellia thrive in shade, and can be used as a backdrop to more seasonal planting that will bring touches of colour into the garden. Alternatively, you may decide to abandon flowers altogether to

GROUND COVER

Acaena spp.
New Zealand burr
Sun **Z5–9**

Ajuga reptans
'Atropurpurea'
Sun **Z3–9**

Alchemilla mollis
Lady's mantle
Shade **Z4–7**

Anthemis cupaniana
Sun **Z5–8**

Arctostaphylos uva-ursi
Bearberry
Sun **Z2–8**

Asarum caudatum
Wild ginger
Shade **Z5–8**

Bergenia spp.
Shade **Z3–8**

Brunnera macrophylla
Siberian bugloss
Shade **Z4–6**

Ceanothus thyrsiflorus
var. *repens*
Californian lilac
Sun **Z7–10**

Cotoneaster spp.
Sun **Z5–8**

Epimedium alpinum
Barrenwort
Shade **Z5–9**

Erica carnea
Winter heath
Sun **Z5–7**

Euonymus fortunei
Sun **Z5–9**

Geranium macrorrhizum
Cranesbill
Shade **Z4–8**

Hebe spp.
Sun **Z8–10**

Helianthemum spp.
Sun rose, rock rose
Sun **Z5–7**

Hypericum calycinum
Rose of Sharon
Sun **Z6–8**

Lamium maculatum
Deadnettle
Shade **Z6–8**

Liriope spp.
Lilyturf
Sun **Z6–10**

Luzula sylvatica
'Marginata'
Greater woodrush
Shade **Z5–9**

Lysimachia nummularia
Creeping Jenny
Sun **Z4–8**

Nepeta
Catmint
Sun **Z4–8**

Ophiopogon spp.
Mondo grass
Sun **Z6–8**

Pachysandra terminalis
Shade **Z4–8**

Phlomis russeliana
Sun **Z4–9**

Polygonum spp.
Knotweed
Sun **Z3–9**

Prunella spp.
Self-heal
Sun **Z5–8**

Pulmonaria spp.
Lungwort
Shade **Z3–8**

Rubus calycinoides
Ornamental bramble
Sun **Z7–8**

Sedum spp.
Stonecrop
Sun **Z4–9**

Stachys byzantina
Bunnies' ears, lamb's tongue
Sun **Z4–9**

Stephanandra incisa
'Crispa'
Sun **Z4–8**

Symphytum grandiflorum
Comfrey
Shade **Z5–9**

Tellima grandiflora
'Purpurea'
Fringecups
Shade **Z4–9**

Tolmiea menziesii
Piggyback plant
Shade **Z6–9**

Vinca spp.
Periwinkle
Shade **Z4–9**

Waldsteinia ternata
Sun **Z4–9**

concentrate on foliage. By planting a few evergreen shrubs with interestingly shaped leaves with shade-loving bamboo and a few unusual perennials and ferns, you can create a peaceful and relaxing haven.

Snails and slugs can become a problem in damp shade. The list of shade-loving plants on page 97 does not include any that are the particular favourites of slugs and snails. However, no matter how wisely you choose your planting, it is unlikely that you will ever have a totally slug-free garden. A number of ways of controlling slugs and snails are listed in Chapter 4 (page 110), and it is advisable to read this chapter before you buy your plants. Dogs and cats can be poisoned by ingesting slug pellets, so anything that will reduce their usage will benefit your pet.

Covering all bare soil will deter dogs and cats from digging. Here, dense mats of heather, hebe and polygonum provide robust ground cover beneath conifers.

GROUND COVER

No matter how well you plan a garden, there are always some empty spaces that are difficult to plant or too small to bother paving. You can gravel these areas, but ground cover will look more attractive, softening larger areas of hard surfaces. Most ground-cover plants are excellent at suppressing weeds and require little maintenance other than a trim with shears at the start of their growing season.

Dense mats of planting will also deter dogs and cats from scratching and digging into the soil or using it as a toilet. In fact, most gardeners who have trouble with cats visiting their garden to do their 'business' are inadvertently inviting them to do so by leaving expanses of bare earth. Ground cover deters visiting cats and has the added advantage of cutting down on weeding. There is a wide range of ground-cover plants available to suit any type of soil or growing condition (see opposite).

You can use ground cover as part of a planting scheme with shrubs and larger perennials, or you can use it to break up the hard edges around paving and gravel. Some species, such as *Vinca major*, may quickly become a nuisance and start to overpower other plants, so it is best to keep such species to the wilder parts of the garden. However, most ground-cover plants are well-behaved, and they can always be removed if they spread too far.

No matter how you use ground cover, you should still observe the basic rules of planting and restrict yourself to a limited number of species that go well together and complement any plants above them. Carefully chosen ground cover can really set off its taller neighbours. The purple bugle, *Ajuga reptans* 'Atropurpurea', is a hardy perennial that will tolerate most growing conditions, including relatively dense shade. It is a beautiful plant with shiny purple foliage and the added benefit of blue flowers in the spring. Plant some snowdrops with it and you will have a stunning display in early spring. I use a number of ground-cover plants with dark foliage, such as *Ophiopogon planiscapus* 'Nigrescens' and ajuga, beneath some yellow-stemmed bamboos to achieve an equally stunning effect.

THE COTTAGE GARDEN

The cottage-garden style typical of many English gardens developed because villagers had small gardens and little money to spend, so they grew plants that were easy to propagate. Clumps of perennials were divided and swapped with neighbours. The result was a jumble of colour made up of hardy perennials, biennials and annuals that were more or less pest-free.

Useful herbs were kept close to the path where they could be picked easily. At the back of the borders, against the fence or the cottage wall, there would be fruit trees or a rambling rose enjoying the warmth of the brickwork. Annuals, such as nigella and godetia, and biennials such as forget-me-nots and sweet williams self-sowed and appeared in unexpected places. This riot of colour would be contained by neatly clipped box hedges (box is remarkably easy to

***Dense planting** with a cottage garden theme, the only drawback being that once the summer display is over, one can be left with little interest over the winter months.*

COTTAGE GARDEN

TREES AND SHRUBS

Buddleia davidii
Butterfly bush **Z5–9**

Buxus spp.
Box **Z6–9**

Cistus spp.
Rock rose **Z7–9**

Clematis spp.
Z5–9

Corylus spp.
Hazel, filbert **Z5–9**

Ilex spp.
Holly **Z4–9**

Lavandula spp.
Lavender **Z6–9**

Lonicera periclymenum
Honeysuckle, woodbine **Z4–9**

Philadelphus spp.
Mock orange **Z5–9**

Rosmarinus officinalis
Rosemary **Z7–9**

Salvia officinalis
Sage **Z7–9**

Syringa villosa
Lilac **Z4–8**

Viburnum spp.
Z4–8

PERENNIALS

Achillea millefolium
Yarrow **Z4–8**

Alchemilla mollis
Lady's mantle **Z4–9**

Astrantia spp.
Masterwort **Z4–8**

Aster spp.
Z3–8

Bergenia spp.
Z3–8

Cynara cardunculus
Cardoon **Z7–9**

Dendranthema spp.
Chrysanthemum **Z4–9**

Dianthus spp.
Pinks **Z4–8**

Geranium spp.
Cranesbill
Z4–8

Heuchera spp.
Z4–8

Lamium spp.
Deadnettle **Z4–8**

Lathyrus latifolius
Perennial pea, everlasting pea **Z5–9**

Nepeta spp.
Catmint **Z5–9**

Paeonia spp.
Peony **Z5–8**

Penstemon spp.
Z6–8

Primula spp.
Primula, polyanthus **Z6–8**

Pulmonaria spp.
Lungwort **Z3–8**

Rudbeckia spp.
Coneflower **Z4–9**

Symphytum spp.
Comfrey **Z4–9**

Verbascum spp.
Mullein **Z5–9**

Veronica spp.
Z5–9

ANNUALS

Eschscholzia californica
Californian poppy **Z5–9**

Godetia spp.
Z5–9

Myosotis spp.
Forget-me-not **Z4–9**

Nicotiana spp.
Tobacco plant **Z5–9**

Nigella damascena
Love-in-a-mist **Z4–9**

propagate) or allowed to spill on to the gravel or cinder paths. Any flowers that become too troublesome were probably snipped off and taken in to brighten up the house.

There are many gardens where this style of planting is still the most appropriate, although these days the result is usually achieved more by careful planning than by happy accident. Needing little more than a mulch of manure in the spring, cottage gardens are easy to maintain and can be remarkably free from pests, especially if you choose disease-resistant varieties of rose. This makes cottage gardens ideal for pets, particularly cats and small, well-behaved dogs. Their only possible drawback is their dependence on perennials and annuals. This can make them uninteresting to both humans and pets during the winter. Today, however, there is a much wider choice of plants than was available to the original cottage gardeners, so it is worth building in some year-round interest as well. This can be achieved by incorporating structural evergreens, such as holly and laurel, or creating a piece of topiary, or by adding larger grasses and perennials that have interesting seedheads. These will add interest throughout the winter, and can easily be cut back once new growth begins in the spring.

ARCHITECTURAL PLANTING

TREES AND SHRUBS
Ailanthus altissima
Tree of heaven **Z6–10**

Aralia elata
Japanese angelica tree
Z6–10

Catalpa bignonioides
Indian bean tree **Z7–9**

Cordyline australis
New Zealand cabbage
palm **Z7–10**

Danäe racemosa
Alexandrian laurel
Z7–9

Eucalyptus spp.
Gum tree **Z7–10**

Fatsia japonica
Japanese aralia
Z8–11

x *Fatshedera lizei*
Z8–11

Magnolia grandiflora
Bull boy
Z7–9

Mahonia spp.
Z5–8

Musa basjoo
Banana **Z10–11**

Phormium tenax
New Zealand flax
Z8–11

Trachycarpus fortunei
Chusan palm **Z7–11**

*Viburnum
rhytidophyllum*
Z6–8

Vitis coignetiae
Crimson glory vine
Z5–9

PERENNIALS
Acanthus spp.
Bear's breeches **Z6–10**

Angelica archangelica
Angelica **Z6–8**

Bergenia spp.
Z4–8

Canna spp.
Indian shot **Z8–10**

Crambe maritima
Sea kale **Z6–9**

Gunnera manicata
Z7–10

Kniphofia spp.
Red-hot poker, torch
lily **Z5–9**

Libertia spp.
Z8–10

Macleaya spp.
Plume poppy **Z4–9**

Rheum palmatum
Ornamental rhubarb
Z5–9

Rodgersia aesculifolia
Z5–8

Sedum spp.
Stonecrop **Z3–10**

FERNS
Phyllitis scolopendrium
Hart's-tongue fern
Z4–8

Dicksonia antarctica
Australian tree fern
Z5–8

*Matteuccia
struthiopteris*
Ostrich fern **Z2–8**

Polystichum munitum
Giant holly fern **Z5–8**

GRASSES
Arundo donax
Giant reed **Z7–10**

BAMBOOS
*Fargesia,
Phyllostachys,
Pseudosasa* spp., *Sasa*
spp. **Z6–10**

Carex buchananii
Leatherleaf sedge
Z6–9

Cortaderia selloana
Pampas grass **Z7–10**

Miscanthus spp.
Z5–10

Stipa gigantea
Golden oats **Z5–10**

Stipa tenuissima
Feather grass **Z7–10**

With simple, robust planting, pet-friendly surfaces and lots of space, even a minimalist garden can be made suitable for a small dog or cat.

ARCHITECTURAL STYLE

The style Western gardeners call modern, minimalist or architectural has been practised by Japanese gardeners for centuries. Japanese garden design is not based on putting things into the garden, but on knowing what to take away – until only the very essence remains. Often this amounts to no more than a few carefully placed rocks set in raked gravel, a single bamboo and some accumulated moss. Although these gardens look nothing like most Western gardens, and as Westerners we may know little about the religion, art or craft that go into making one of these great gardens, we somehow instinctively know that to add anything else would spoil it completely.

Since the early part of the 20th century, minimalist values and principles have permeated Western art and design, becoming part of our everyday lives. The early pioneers of the Modernist movement, such as Mies van der Rohe, Walter Gropius and Le Corbusier, made

use of the latest technology and new materials such as reinforced concrete. This allowed them to create new shapes and forms. Spaces could be bigger and less cluttered. For the most part, the commissions these architects received were for civic buildings and institutions, but a few Modernist homes were surrounded by equally Modernist gardens. Interior design was carried over into the garden by extending flooring materials such as tiling into patio and seating areas. Indoors and outdoors were seamlessly joined, separated only by expanses of glazing. Space and simplicity abounded, with plants being chosen strictly because of shape and form.

Such aesthetics do not prevent minimalist gardens from being pet-friendly. Planting will probably be dense and repetitive, so there are unlikely to be expanses of bare soil. However, surround a piece of sculpture with a sea of silver sand and your cat will happily use it as a toilet. Just take care to filter the sand before your designer friends turn up for dinner. Likewise beds filled with wafting grasses will be a favourite playground for any cat. If you plant a single architectural shrub such as a yucca or a cordyline against an expanse of blank wall, insert some geometric blocks that protrude from the surface to give your cat an easy route up to the top of the wall.

With dense planting and raised beds surrounded by rendered brickwork and stone chipping, paving or concrete slabs instead of lawn, the minimalist garden has little for a dog to damage. Unfortunately it is unlikely that there will be much to entertain a dog either, and a kennel may spoil the effect. If you want to combine an architectural garden and a dog, stick to toy breeds such as miniature dachshunds that require limited exercise.

THE OUTDOOR ROOM

All over the world, houses and gardens are tending to become smaller. Many people have gardens 10-m (33-ft) square or smaller. If a garden of this size is treated traditionally with lawns, borders and other horticultural features, it will become crowded and unpleasing. With smaller gardens, instead of following traditional design approaches, it is a good idea to focus on the idea of the garden as an outdoor room. You would not start decorating and furnishing a room indoors without having thought about how the space is going to be used, and you should apply the same principles outside.

Gardens are primarily for people and their pets to enjoy, and there are many ways of achieving this. You might decide to create a dense jungle that is packed to the brim with interesting plants and has little else but a small space to sit, so that you can wander around tending to plants at the end of a busy day and your cat can have its own jungle. However, many people would find it a chore to have such a garden and would prefer one that requires little maintenance, and where plants are only one element. No matter what solution you adopt, the key to success is a clear idea of how you want to use the space and then a bold, simple design.

PLANTING IN GRAVEL

If pea gravel is laid too deep it is difficult and deeply uncomfortable to walk on. If the earth is firm and well-consolidated, cover it with a semi-permeable membrane that will allow water to drain through it while suppressing weeds. Lay 5 cm (2 in) of gravel on top. Alternatively, get rid of all the weeds, then spread a layer of hardcore and ram it down hard to provide a firm base. On top, add a second layer of smaller hardcore, such as hoggin, and ram this down hard as well. Now add the top layer of pea gravel. This may result in a covering that is up to 30 cm (12 in) thick, but you can still plant directly into it.

Clare Palgrave relaxes in the Pet-Friendly Garden she exhibited at the Hampton Court Palace Flower Show in 1997. A modest outdoor room of 8 m by 8 m (26 ft by 26 ft), it contained many pet-friendly features. Details of the garden can be found on pages 66–71.

PLANTING IN GRAVEL

SHRUBS
Ballota spp.
Helichrysum
italicum
Lavandula spp.
Lotus hirsuitum
Phormium tenax
Santolina spp.
Senecio spp.

PERENNIALS AND GRASSES
Alchemilla mollis
Ophiopogon
planiscarpus

Phalaris
arundinacea
Phlomis russeliana
Sisyrinchium spp.
Stachys byzantina
Verbascum spp.

ANNUALS
Eschscholzia
californica
Limnanthes
douglasii
Myosotis spp.
Tropaeolum majus

ALPINES
Acaena spp.
Aubretia spp.
Cotula spp.
Hypericum
olympicum
Sempervivum
montanum
Thymus spp.

Two of the most common poisonous plants that it is best to avoid. Deadly nightshade, Atropa belladonna *(top) and foxglove,* Digitalis purpurea *(bottom).*

Trees and shrubs are best planted in their dormant period. Water the plant thoroughly to soften the root ball. Rake away the gravel and dig a hole that is at least 10 cm (4 in) wider and deeper than the existing container. Pile the earth and rubble on to a piece of heavy-duty plastic sheeting. Remove all the rubble. Turn the remaining soil, incorporating some compost. Loosen the roots of a pot-bound plant and place it in the hole. The stem should be at the same level with the earth as it was in the pot. Backfill and firm down the surface. Water the plant well until it is established. As long as they get some moisture, many plants will thrive in gravel. Some will self-seed, while others spread their roots through the gravel. These plants will soften the surface and need little care, other than removing any that are getting out of hand.

PLANTS TO AVOID

Although it is uncommon, dogs and cats can eat poisonous plants and make themselves ill. Rabbits, too, may nibble anything that looks green and inviting. If your garden already contains poisonous plants, or if you add more from the garden centre, your pets will be at risk.

Plants vary in their toxicity: many are irritant rather than poisonous. Make a list of all existing plants in the garden and check it for poisonous ones. You may decide that a few irritant species will not be a serious risk to your cat or dog, but it is unwise to let a rabbit

wander freely in the flowerbeds until you are sure that all toxic plants have been removed. In the UK plants are divided into three groups, according to their toxicity. Most good nurseries and garden centres will label plants and bulbs that are toxic or cause skin allergies. The following plants are the ones you are most likely to come across:

Aconitum (monkshood) is a hardy perennial growing to about 1.5 m (5 ft). The most common varieties have spires of blue flowers in the summer, though yellow and white varieties can be found. Every part of the plant is poisonous and should be handled with great care. Its name is derived from the Greek *akon*, meaning a dart, and refers to a time when arrow tips were dipped in the plant's deadly juices.

Atropa belladonna (deadly nightshade) is a herbaceous perennial with poisonous black berries. It grows in the wild and can easily find its way into a rural garden.

Laburnum is a genus of hardy deciduous trees that are covered with racemes of yellow flowers in summer. All species are poisonous.

Ricinus communis (castor-oil plant) is a fast-growing annual that was widely used in Victorian and Edwardian gardens in Britain as a centrepiece in formal bedding, and is becoming popular in tropical planting schemes. The seeds of the plant contain a powerful poison known as ricin.

Daphne mezereum is a deciduous flowering shrub that is covered with fragrant pink blossoms early in the season. These are followed

POISONOUS PLANTS

CATEGORY A
Poisonous. Can cause severe blistering dermatitis if they come into contact with skin.

Rhus radicans
Poison ivy

Rhus succedanea
Wax tree

Rhus verniciflua
Varnish tree

Rhus vernix
Poison sumac

CATEGORY B
Toxic if eaten, causing nausea and vomiting. Those marked with an asterisk may also cause a skin allergy.

Aconitum
Monkshood, wolfsbane, aconite

Arum*
Cuckoo pint

Atropa
Deadly nightshade

Colchicum
Autumn crocus, meadow saffron, naked ladies

Convallaria majaris
Lily-of-the-valley

Daphne laureola,
D. mezereum and other species
Mezereon, spurge laurel

Datura syn.
Brugsmansia
Angels' trumpets

Dictamnus albus*
Burning bush

Dieffenbachia*
Dumb cane, leopard lily

Digitalis
Foxglove

x *Gaulnettya*

Gloriosa superba
Glory lily

Hysocyamus niger
Henbane

Laburnum
Golden chain

Lantana

Nerium oleander
Oleander, rosebay

Phytolacca americana
Pokeroot, pokeweed, red-ink plant

Primula obconica*
German primula, poisonous primula

Ricinus communis
Castor-oil plant

Ruta*
Rue

Solanum dulcamara
Bittersweet, woody nightshade

Taxus
Yew

Veratrum
False hellebore

CATEGORY C
Harmful if eaten in quantity. Those marked with an asterisk may also cause a skin allergy.

Aesculus
Horse chestnut, buckeye

Agrostemma
Corn cockle

Alstroemeria*
Peruvian lily

Anemone
Windflower

Aquilegia
Columbine, granny's bonnets

Argemone
Prickly poppy, devil's fig

Asclepias
Milkweed, silkweed

Caltha
Kingcup, marsh marigold

by poisonous red berries, which will cause nausea and vomiting.

Digitalis (foxglove), is a hardy biennial that self-seeds all over the garden. It contains digitalis, a powerful drug that has long been used as a heart stimulant.

Nerium oleander is a tender evergreen shrub that bears clusters of fragrant red flowers. If the thick, lance-shaped leaves are bruised, they secrete a poisonous juice.

POISONOUS PLANTS

Catharanthus roseus
Rose periwinkle

Convolvulus
Dwarf morning glory

Cupressocyparis x
leylandii*
Leyland cypress

Cytisus battanderia
Moroccan broom,
Pineapple broom

Delphinium

Dendrathema*

Echium*

Euonymus europaeus,
E. japonicus
European spindle,
Japanese spindle

Euphorbia*
Spurge, Milkweed

Fremontodendron
Flannel flower

Gaultheria

Hedera
Ivy

Helleborus
Lenten rose, Christmas
rose

Hyacinthus*
Hyacinth

Hypericum perforatum

Ipomoea
Morning glory

Iris

Juniperus sabina
Savin

Kalmia
Mountain laurel, calico
bush

Lathyrus odoratus
Sweet pea

Ligustrum
Privet

Lilium
Lily

Linum
Flax

Lobelia tupa*

Lupinus
Lupin

Malva
Mallow

Narcissus*
Daffodil

Nicotiana
Tobacco plant

Ornithogalum
Star-of-Bethlehem,
starflower

Papaver
Poppy

Polygonatum
Solomon's seal

Prunus laurocerasus
Laurel, Cherry laurel

Pulsatilla vulgaris
Pasque flower

Rhamnus
Buckthorn

Schefflera*

Scilla
Bluebell, Squill

Thalictrum
Meadow rue

Thuja*
Arborvitae

Tulipa*
Tulip

Wisteria

Maintaining your pet-friendly garden

Wherever possible, particularly when pets are about, it is better to try to avoid using chemicals to maintain your garden. There are a number of environmentally friendly sprays available for the control of pests, but try to use these in the evening to avoid harming bees.

Likewise there is a wide range of organic fertilizers available. If you are intent on being totally green, you can use animal manure as a fertilizer. Alternatively, you can make your own fertilizer by growing a crop of comfrey. Harvest the leaves, squash them down in a barrel, activate them with a little urine, and cover them with water. After four or five weeks, they rot down to form a black concentrated solution that smells absolutely horrible. Once diluted, though, it forms a perfectly balanced liquid feed for many crops and plants.

Using disease- and pest-resistant plants such as these hardy geraniums, cistus *and* eschscholzia *will help you keep your use of garden chemicals to a minimum.*

PEST-RESISTANT PLANTING

No garden can ever be totally pest-free, but there are steps that you can take to limit their appearance. Remove any dead or diseased plant material before it can become a home for pests. Check all new plants you acquire to make sure that they are healthy and free from disease. Healthy plants are much more resistant to disease than plants that are struggling to survive. If you try to grow a plant in a position that is not to its liking, not only will it become sickly, it is also likely to become diseased or infested by a pest. Look out for plants that are not doing well, and check that they are in a suitable situation. Remove caterpillars and weeds as soon as you see them. Try to restrict your planting to hardy, disease-resistant plants, and varieties that will flourish on your soil.

There are a number of pest-resistant plants that are suitable for growing in the pet-friendly garden, and they are listed on page 113. Plants such as roses and hostas are very difficult to grow without recourse to chemical pesticides, but if you cannot do without them, consult a specialist book and try to choose a disease- or pest-resistant

Keeping to plants that thrive in your soil will mean you use fewer chemicals. Here hardy geranium and the yellow-leaved Escallonia laevis 'Gold Brian' thrive on alkaline soil where acid-loving plants such as rhododendrons would be difficult to grow.

Hostas are always proned to slugs, but those with thicker, ribbed foliage such as Hosta 'Sum and Substance' are reputed to be less prone to attack.

variety. *Rosa rugosa* is known for its disease-resistant qualities, and survives the summer with little visible pest damage. Hostas with thicker, ribbed foliage such as *H.* 'Sum and Substance' and *H. tardiana* 'Halcyon' are reputed to be less attractive to slugs. Alternatively you can plant a hosta in a hanging basket, add water-retaining pellets to keep it damp, and water the basket regularly. You should be rewarded with a good display of perfect foliage.

MECHANICAL TRAPS

Mechanical traps are only limited by your ingenuity. In my childhood, we always had a jam pot half full of diluted jam hanging in the plum tree. The wasps crawled in through a small hole in the lid and were unable to get out. You should never bait such traps with honey or use them near flowers, otherwise you are likely to trap friendly bees as well. An old-fashioned flypaper hung in a greenhouse will trap vast numbers of whitefly and thrip.

You can try mulching round plants that are susceptible to leaf damage with sharp gravel, pine needles, crushed, baked eggshells, and beard trimmings taken from an electric razor.

PET-FRIENDLY PLANTS RESISTANT TO SLUGS AND SNAILS

While no plant is totally immune to damage by slugs and snails, these herbaceous plants should survive relatively unscathed. Some grow so quickly that their foliage does not have time to get damaged. Others, like *Alchemilla mollis*, have hairy leaves and tend to be ignored. Some contain natural chemicals that make them taste unpleasant to slugs and snails.

Acanthus mollis
  (Bear's breeches)
Agapanthus spp.
Alchemilla mollis
  (Lady's mantle)
Anemone hupehenis
Anemone x *hybrida*
Antirrhinum majus
  (Snapdragon)

Armeria spp.
Aster amellus
Aster x *frikartii*,
  A. novae-angliae
  (Aster)
Astilbe x *arendsii*
Astrantia major
  (Masterwort)
Bergenia spp.
Centaurea dealbata,
  C. montana
  (Knapweed)
Corydalis lutea
Cynara cardunculus
  (Cardoon)
Dicentra spectabilis
Eryngium spp.
  (Sea holly)
Foeniculum vulgare
  (Fennel)
Fuchsia cultivars
Gaillardia aristata
  (Blanket flower)
Geranium spp.
  (Cranesbill)
Geum chiloense
  (Avens)
Hemerocallis cultivars
  (Daylily)

Liatris spicata
  (Gayfeathers)
Lysimachia punctata
  (Garden loosestrife)
Myosotis spp.
  (Forget-me-not)
Nepeta x *faassenii*
  (Catmint)
Papaver nudicaule
  (Iceland poppy)
Papaver orientale
  (Oriental poppy)
Pelargonium spp.
  (Geranium)
Phlox paniculata
Physostegia
  virginiana
  (Obedient plant)
Polemonium
  foliosissimum
  (Jacob's ladder)
Polygonum spp.
  (Knotweed)
Potentilla hybrids and
  cultivars
Pulmonaria spp.
  (Lungwort)
Rudbeckia fulgida
  (Black-eyed Susan)

Salvia nemorosa or
  Salvia x *superba*
  (Sage)
Saxifraga x *urbium*
  (London pride)
Scabiosa caucasica
  (Scabious)
Sedum spectabile
  (Ice plant)
Sempervivum spp.
  (Houseleek)
Sisyrinchium spp.
Solidago spp.
  (Golden rod)
Stachys macrantha
Tanacetum coccineum
  (Pyrethrum)
Thalictrum
  aquilegiifolium
  (Meadow rue)
Tradescantia
  virginiana
  (Spiderwort)
Tropaeolum spp.
  (Nasturtium)
Verbascum spp.
  (Mullein)
Ornamental grasses
  and sedges

If you place the upturned skins of fruits such as grapefruit and melon between susceptible plants, snails and slugs will use them as refuges during the day. Try to remember to empty them once or twice during the day, and you will soon start to reduce pest numbers. From an aesthetic point of view, the green skins of ogen melons and watermelons are less intrusive than the bright yellow skins of cantaloupe melons or grapefruit.

Earwigs, and other creeping things that like safe, secure places to rest, can be lured into an upturned, straw-filled plant pot on the end of a cane. You need to remove the pot occasionally and tap the contents into a polythene bag so the insects can be disposed of before they head back into your dahlias.

French marigolds

planted amongst salad and vegetable crops attract hoverflies that will devour aphids. Besides helping reduce the need for chemicals, marigolds also add colour to the vegetable plot.

Placing beer traps underneath plants seems to work well. An old cup pressed into the soil and filled with any type of beer is alluring to any passing mollusc. Keep the rim 12 mm ($^1/_2$ in) above the soil to prevent beetles and other beneficial insects from inadvertently falling in. The slugs are attracted by the smell of the beer, fall in and drown. You need to empty and top up the cups regularly, and will need a large number of traps to control a sizeable infestation.

COMPANION PLANTING

If you grow large patches of any vegetable or flower, you may well find that you have effectively set out a feast for passing pests.

COMPANION PLANTING TIPS

French marigolds planted between rows of potatoes will help to protect them from eelworms. Planted with almost any other crop, they will attract hoverflies, which devour aphids.

Growing carrots and onions together confuses carrot and onion flies, which are unable to distinguish separate scents.

Aromatic herbs, such as chives, catmint, thyme and parsley, planted between rose bushes, deter aphids as well as providing a fragrant ground cover.

Planting one or two basil plants with tomatoes and sweet peppers helps to ward off whitefly.

Ladybirds prey on pests such as aphids, and should be encouraged in the garden.

However, if you plant vulnerable vegetables and flowers together with their natural companion plant, pests that would normally demolish your crop will usually fly past. Typically, the companion is an aromatic plant; it is believed that its scent prevents insects being able to smell the crop that the plant is protecting. At the same time, many companion plants actually attract beneficial insects that will prey on pests. Dill and fennel, for example, attract hoverflies, which in turn prey on aphids. Because companion planting obviates the need for chemicals, and because the companion plants seem to alter the composition of the soil, it has the added bonus of enriching your garden. You will find many examples of companion planting in any book on organic gardening, but some of the most common combinations are given on page 115.

ENCOURAGING PREDATORS

Ladybirds are well known aphid predators. Hoverflies, lacewings and wasps will also help to control aphids, caterpillars and other pests. However, the number of helpful predators in the average garden is usually far smaller than the number of pests. If you want to increase your local population of predators, you should grow the plants they like to use for feeding and breeding. Camomile, cosmos, golden rod and yarrow will attract lacewings and marigolds; fennel and yarrow will attract ladybirds. There are many other species that will attract useful predators, not to mention bees, butterflies and birds – all of which add interest to the garden.

HANDWORK

It is quite possible to keep a small garden free of slugs, snails and other pests by becoming a hunter yourself. Done in the right frame of mind, this is not quite the chore that it may sound. Walking round the garden after dusk on any evening of the year can be a joy. If you have been at work all day, there is nothing more rewarding than taking the time to look at the new growth or enjoy some of the scents. But try not to get too carried away because there is work to be done.

You will need a torch and a plastic bag. If you are squeamish, you may also need a pair of rubber gloves. Look under the leaves of all the plants that are favourites of slugs and snails. Remember snails can climb to considerable heights and also attack trees and shrubs. In my garden, snails are drawn towards the soft leaves of a Moroccan broom, *Cytisus battandieri*. Despite having little foliage near the ground and being 4 m (13 ft) high, the snails climb up into the branches and it is not unusual to find as many snails above my head as beneath my feet.

To dispose of your snails, tie a knot in your plastic bag to prevent your captives from escaping, then drop them in the garbage. Alternatively, collect them in a container and despatch them by adding water that has just gone off the boil.

Another pest that can be controlled by regular night-time patrols is the vine weevil (*Otiorhynchus sulcatus*). You may not know that you have this pest unless you know what you are looking for. The larvae feed on the roots of plants, causing them to wilt and collapse. The adult black beetle makes semicircular indentations round the edges of leaves. If you shine your torch into the plant you can frequently find the adult weevil climbing about. They are unable to fly and, once disturbed, will try to make their escape by dropping to the ground.

To foil them, put one hand a few centimetres below the weevil before knocking it gently off the plant with the other hand. Drop the weevil on a hard surface, such as paving, and put your foot on it. You can also try to catch the adults by placing a loosely rolled piece of corrugated cardboard on the soil round damaged plants. Weevils sleep during the day, and you will find them hiding in your cardboard. You can also control vine weevils by adding a pathogenic nematode (see page 118) to the soil round damaged plants in the warmer summer months. If you have a prized specimen growing in a container, you can protect it by standing the pot on bricks in the middle of a large tray of water. Vine weevils are incapable of flight and steer clear of water, so the plant will be entirely protected.

It is quite easy to control weeds in paths by pulling out any new intruder before it has the chance to self-seed. Going over a flowerbed regularly with a hoe will also keep weeds down. However, if you want to control pests and weeds by hand, you need to be diligent, and to make your night-time circuit of the garden part of your daily routine. The neighbours will soon get used to seeing you on your twilight patrol.

A snail feasts on the soft leaves of Cytisus battandieri, *but can readily be plucked away from its snack by the night-time snail hunter!*

USING CHEMICALS

Unfortunately, even if you try to limit your use of chemical herbicides, pesticides, or fertilizers, it is likely that you will be driven to resort to them at some time or other. It is almost impossible to grow some plants without using pesticides: roses, for example, are prone to black spot and mildew and need to be sprayed regularly throughout the summer. Hostas are a favourite food of slugs and, unless you apply slug pellets, or diligently resort to some other control mechanism, their luscious leaves can soon become tattered skeletons.

If possible, grow plants that require treating with chemicals in an area of the garden that can be made pet-free. A front garden is ideal for this.

USING PEST AND WEED CONTROLS SAFELY

Many chemicals, especially rodent and slug poisons, are a hazard to pets because the pet can find them just as tasty as the intended victims. If you plan to use any of the products listed below, follow these safety precautions. Remember that visiting cats and dogs will also need to be protected.

Rat and mouse poison

Controlling infestations of rats and mice is perhaps best left to the professionals, but if you do it yourself, you should exercise great care and follow the manufacturer's instructions. Many poisons contain warfarin, which causes death by internal bleeding. If your pet

eats rat or mouse poison, you should take it to your vet immediately. There is an antidote, but it needs to be administered without delay.

If you resort to mousetraps or rat-traps in a shed or outhouse, you should keep the doors and windows locked at all times, otherwise you might catch a cat by the paw rather than a rat by the tail. There are rodent traps available that catch the animals alive, but while you may be happy to release a mouse back into a nearby field, it takes a brave person to deal with a full-grown rat.

Slug bait

One of the most frequent causes of poisoning seen by vets is slug pellets. They usually contain metaldehyde, which is very attractive to cats and dogs and for which there is no specific antidote. It causes severe fits, and although your vet can give sedatives, anaesthetics and intravenous fluids in an attempt to control the seizures, often the pet dies.

If you have to use slug bait, be careful. If you scatter it all over the place, your pet could easily find a pellet and eat it – with dire consequences. It is better to place a few small piles round susceptible plants, covering each one with a slate or tile propped up with a large

PROTECTING YOUR PETS

Most chemicals carry instructions on their preparation, administration and storage. Follow the manufacturer's directions, and keep your pet confined in the house for the recommended length of time after you have used the chemical. By far the greatest hazard for a pet is finding undiluted fluids or powders in an open container. Empty and clean containers thoroughly after use, and ensure that unused chemicals are stored out of reach of animals and children. A high shelf may keep dangerous products out of a dog's way, but a cat can gain access to most places. The safest storage place is a locked cupboard.

If you suspect your pet has been poisoned by chemicals, follow the instructions on page 120.

pebble. That way, the slugs and snails can get to the bait, but your pet is relatively safe.

Pathogenic nematodes
Instead of using slug bait, you could try killing slugs and snails by applying the pathogenic nematode, Phasmarhabditis hermaphrodita. *It has to be applied fresh and is generally only available by mail order. When it arrives it looks like a pack of mud, but actually contain millions of minute, wormlike creatures. You mix the pack with water and apply it to the soil when the temperature is 10°C (50°F) or above. Slugs bury themselves in the soil during the day; the*

nematodes to enter their bodies and infect them with a bacterium, which kills them within a few days. Treatment with a nematode can free your garden from slugs for six weeks or more. However, because snails spend most of their time above ground, they are generally less affected.

Liquid soap
You can spray aphids with liquid soap. This is now available at many garden centres, but you can also make your own with a stiff solution of concentrated washing-up liquid.

Herbicides
There is a wide range of weed-killers and herbicides available. All are clearly labelled and many have specific instructions about what to do with your cat or dog while you are applying the chemical and for days afterwards.

Paraquat is a commonly used herbicide and is worth mentioning separately as ingestion by pets causes death by liver failure. There are other less toxic herbicides available, so paraquat is best avoided. As with all garden chemicals, herbicides should be stored under lock and key in a cupboard.

Common hazards and first aid

POISONING

If your pet brushes against a recently sprayed plant, its coat will become contaminated with the chemical. The pet will then lick its coat in an attempt to clean itself. Cats and dogs may also ingest garden chemicals used to kill pests and weeds. The visible signs of poisoning are varied, but commonly include vomiting, diarrhoea, convulsions and paralysis. Contact a veterinary surgeon immediately and arrange for an emergency examination. If you have time, wash your pet with a mild human hair shampoo, rinse and dry it thoroughly. Wrap it up warmly and take it to the vet. If you think you know which poison is involved, take the container with you, as this will help your vet determine the appropriate treatment. Your vet may use an emetic to make your pet vomit, a laxative to hurry the substance through its intestines or a demulcent to protect its stomach lining.

STINGS

Puppies are naturally curious and want to investigate everything. Cats are born hunters and will play with anything that moves. As a result, it is not unusual for pets to be stung by wasps and bees during the summer. The sting is often around the head, mouth or front paws. The pet will suddenly yelp or miaow in pain and paw or lick the sting, which will soon start to swell up at an alarming rate. If the sting is in the mouth or the throat, the pet may start to experience difficulty in breathing. This can be life-threatening, so rush your pet to the nearest veterinary surgery for immediate treatment.

When a bee stings, the sting is usually left in and the bee dies. Withdraw the sting with tweezers, if possible, and wash the area with bicarbonate of soda, as the sting is acid and you need to neutralize it. Wasps withdraw their stings and can repeat the attack. Bathe the area in vinegar, as the sting is alkaline. If your pet is still in distress, contact your vet without delay.

Bleeding

Dogs and cats can injure themselves in the garden. Bleeding that is not checked can soon lead to shock and may result in death. You can try to check bleeding from a surface wound by applying pressure to the bleeding point with your thumb, or by placing a wad of cotton wool over the wound and bandaging it tightly. If the bleeding continues, apply another bandage over the top.

If the wound is in a leg or in the tail, apply a tourniquet. Tear off a narrow piece of cloth and tie it tightly between the wound and the pet's heart. Insert a pencil or piece of stick beneath the knot and twist until the bleeding stops. Contact your veterinary surgery immediately. While a tourniquet is usually very effective in stopping bleeding, it should not be used for more than 15 minutes at a time.

Snake bites

If you live in snake country you have to accept that one may find its way into your garden, or that your dog may come across one on a walk. Unless it has had any previous experience of snakes, your dog will be naturally curious and will investigate with its nose. This means that most snake bites are either on the face or on the legs. Symptoms of snake bites include drooling and trembling; your dog's pupils may also appear dilated.

First, apply an ice pack or some cold water to slow down the flow of blood round the bite. A bag of frozen vegetables from the freezer is usually the quickest thing to grab. Contact your veterinary surgery at once so they can prepare an anti-venom injection before you arrive.

If the dog has been bitten on its paw, wrap a tourniquet round the leg between the bite and the heart to try to delay the spread of the venom. Keep the dog as still as possible, and carry it to and from the car if you drive to the veterinary surgery: if its heart rate increases the venom will spread more quickly round the body.

Pets and gardens through the ages

Until about a hundred years ago, most domesticated animals were a source of food, or were expected to work for their keep. Exotic animals and birds were often collected for the pleasure of kings and emperors – the rulers of the Chinese, Indian and Egyptian empires all kept animals in garden menageries, which were forerunners of the modern zoo. But it is only in comparatively recent times that animals have become household pets, with a whole industry dedicated to keeping them fed, groomed, comfortable and entertained.

Until a hundred years ago, the land around most dwellings would be for crops, livestock and keeping bees for honey, as this illustration by the medieval painter Französiseche Buchmalerei shows. The cat shown at the feet of one of the women was probably valued as much for keeping vermin under control as it was for being a companion animal.

Many ancient cultures venerated certain animals. The ancient Egyptians, for example, viewed the cat as sacred, and often embalmed cats when they died. The Minoans created a cult around the bull and practised the dangerous sport of bull-leaping. Myths and legends invested animals with magical or mystical powers. European witches, for example, were often depicted with black cats, which were believed to have magic powers. Our modern bond with pet animals is a continuation of this ancient relationship between human and animal. From the New York socialite who takes her toy poodle to the grooming parlour every week, to the Australian aborigine who hunts with his dog in the heart of the outback, many humans feel the need to bond with a pet.

VICTORIAN PET-OWNERS

Pet ownership was made popular in Britain by the Victorians. With fortunes built on coal, cotton and wool, wealthy Victorians built elaborate stables for their horses and exquisite kennels for their dogs, in all manner of architectural styles. Huge glasshouses and winter gardens were stocked with exotic plants and birds. Even humble city-dwellers indulged their pets when the opportunity arose. The lakes in Victoria Park in east London were frequently used for swimming and bathing, and it was not unknown for 3,000 people to take to the waters at any one time. Dogs were also allowed to swim in the lakes,

and owners took them to the park to be washed. Eventually dogs had to be banned from the western ornamental lake, because they were creating a nuisance.

This indulgence did not appear to extend to adapting estates or gardens for a pet's benefit, however, though this does not mean that animals had no influence on the features of gardens and the surrounding landscape. Most families reared their crops and livestock near their houses and, although we do not think of them as important sources of food today, bees, doves and rabbits were a common feature in many gardens.

Dogs used for sport often had fine kennels built for them next to some of England's great country houses. The hound kennels built by Sir Lancelot Allgood in 1768, at Nunwick in Northumberland, were designed to look like a romantic ruin when viewed from the house. At Milton, near Peterborough, the hounds are still kennelled in a sham ruin attributed both to Sir William Chambers and Humphrey Repton. Belvoir Castle in Rutland also has a magnificent kennel that is still in use.

BENIFICENT BEES

Until 200 years ago, sugar was unknown in Europe and honey was used as a sweetener. Honey was also fermented to produce mead, which was the most widely available alcoholic drink. Bees, therefore, were very important, not only for the production of honey, but also for the production of beeswax, which was used to make writing tablets and candles.

Hives constructed from all manner of materials were a common sight in many gardens. Skeps (baskets for bees) were usually made of straw, but wicker, willow, hazel, grass, reed and sedge were also used. To make the hives waterproof they were thatched, or daubed with cow-dung and covered with ashes, sand or gravel.

Honey and mead were prized and beehives were a common sight in much of Europe.

Beeboles were niches in walls or buildings into which hives could be placed to protect them from the worst of the weather. Packwood House in Warwickshire is renowned for having no fewer than 30 beeboles, set in pairs into a 17th-century wall that divides the terrace from the yew garden. The wall has a small gazebo at either end. One of these contains a long fireplace, which was used to warm the peach trees growing up the wall behind it, stimulating the production of blossom and nectar for the bees to collect. Beeboles were not considered a luxury and could also be found in more modest homes.

There were other ways of sheltering skeps: in the grounds of Gloucestershire College of Agriculture at Hartpury is the oldest known beehouse in England, said to date from before 1500. This building is 9 m (30 ft) long and 2.5 m (8 ft) high, and contains niches for 33 skeps. It is made entirely of stone, mostly quarried from Caen in Normandy, and used to stand in the gardens of Minchinhampton Manor near Nailsworth, before being moved to its current location in 1968. The manor was granted to the Abbaye aux Dames by William the Conqueror and Queen Matilda in the 11th century, and for 500 years rents and dues were paid to the Abbess. One of them must have sent over this wonderful structure topped with crosses, put there to reflect the belief that honey came from heaven and that bees were merely the method of delivering this precious gift to man.

The gardens of Hall Place near Hurley in Berkshire, now the Berkshire College of Agriculture, and Attingham Park in Shropshire both contain elaborate timber bee houses. The one at

Straw beehives set in *the beeboles in the wall of the garden of Packwood House, Warwickshire.*

Hurley is distinctly Chinese in design, and was probably made from an early 19th-century architect's pattern book; the one at Attingham is thought to date from the 18th century. Besides being highly decorative, these bee houses were very practical in that the hives could be tended from behind, something that was not possible with stone beeboles. As sugar and wine became more widely available in the middle of the 19th century, beekeeping gradually declined.

PIGEONS AND DOVES FOR DINNER

Doves and pigeons were symbols of love, peace and fertility in ancient Greece and Rome. The flamboyant courtship ritual of the cocks led to them being viewed as sacred, and they were frequently sacrificed in temples. Pigeons and doves were also widely eaten – as long ago as 2,500 BC the Egyptians dined on both.

In the Middle Ages, pigeons and doves formed an important part of people's diet, especially in winter, when food tended to be scarce. In medieval France only the aristocracy was allowed to keep doves and pigeons, so many dovecotes were torn down during the French Revolution. French dovecotes tended to be very ornate; the best surviving examples can be found in the grounds of abbeys and priories, which escaped the rampages of the mob.

The idea of keeping doves and pigeons in dovecotes and lofts appears to have been introduced to Britain at the time of the Norman Conquest. These cotes were simple, functional structures made from local materials. Some were massive, capable of housing 500 pairs of birds. It is estimated that there were 26,000 dovecotes in Britain during the 17th century, making them a common sight. Their numbers began to decline when root crops were introduced in the 18th century. These crops made it possible to feed large numbers of cattle through the winter months, thus providing an alternative and more nutritious food supply. Other than being used for carrying messages, pigeons became purely decorative or, with the advent of pigeon racing, sporting.

Reputedly the oldest dovecote in England, now in a private garden in Hurley, Berkshire, this is said to date from 1307.

Many dovecotes survive. Herefordshire is full of little black-and-white, post-and-truss dovehouses: Launtely Court, Kings Pyon and Bidney Farm are particularly fine examples, all within a few kiliometres of each other. At Hurley in Berkshire, there is a large dovecote some 24 m (80 ft) in diameter, said to date from 1307 and reputed to be the oldest in England. It has a fine working example of a potence (a revolving ladder mounted on a central post), which

provides access to the 600 nests set in the circular wall. A dovecote of a similar age and design survives at Garway in Herefordshire.

By the middle of the 18th century dovecotes were in decline because people had became only too aware of the damage the birds did to crops. Any dovecote built after this date was designed to be as decorative as it was functional. Cliveden in Berkshire – at various times the home of the Dukes of Sutherland and Westminster, and later the Astor family – has a pepper-pot dovecote attributed to Henry

Clutton. Built during the 1860s, at the same time as the extravagantly decorated clock tower across the lawn, the dovecote forms a corner of the urn-topped walls that run parallel to the drive and add grandeur to the approach.

The eccentric composer, artist and aesthete Lord Berners (1883–1950) was fond of doves, which formed part of the menagerie at his home in Farringdon, to the west of Oxford. There is no record that he let them into the house, which is a liberty he allowed to his pet horse. However, he did dye them pink and blue. They must have been a wonderful sight swooping through the English countryside in the early 20th century.

RABBITS: FROM POT TO PET

Although rabbits originally came from the plains of the Iberian peninsula, it was the Romans who first started keeping them in captivity for meat production. Gradually, they were introduced into northern Europe, and became widespread in Britain after the Norman Conquest, having been kept in warrens throughout medieval France. By the middle of the 15th century, the rabbit had spread throughout Britain. Reportedly, some 4,000 conies were part of the feast that celebrated the appointment of the Archbishop of York and the Chancellor of England in 1465.

By the end of the Middle Ages, domesticated rabbits were widely kept, some having been selectively bred to create different colours. Many were housed in a rabbit pit, which was little more than a warren enclosed by a high retaining wall. By the beginning of the 18th century, rabbit owners began to realize that keeping rabbits warm and dry in hutches encouraged them to breed in winter, when a higher price could be obtained for their meat. Keeping rabbits became a lucrative business – even the droppings became highly valuable as fertilizer. No wonder then that, by the mid-19th century, many of the rural and urban poor were keeping hutch rabbits in their gardens and back yards.

In the 1890s, Belgian hares became very popular in the US. This fad seems to have been fuelled by breeders who offered to buy back the reared animals at an almost guaranteed price. Rabbit farms were established in the Midwest, causing uproar among the local

This Roman fresco detail shows a Cupid hunting a rabbit. Rabbits remained an important source of meat right up until the 1950s.

EPITAPH TO A HARE

Here lies, whom hound did
	ne'er pursue,
Nor swifter greyhound follow,
Whose foot ne'er tainted
	morning dew,
Nor ear heard the huntsman's
	halloo.

Old Tiney, surliest of his kind,
Who nursed with tender care,
And to domestic bounds
	confined,
Was still a wild jack-hare.

Though duly from my hand
	he took
His pittance every night
He did it with a jealous look
And, when he could, would
	bite.

His diet was of wheaten
	bread,
And milk, and oats, and
	straw;
Thistles or lettuces instead,
With sand to scour his maw.

On twigs of hawthorn he
	regaled;
On pippins' russet peel,
And, when his juicy salads
	fail'd,
Sliced carrot pleased him well.

A Turkey carpet was his lawn,
Whereon he loved to bound,
To skip and gambol like a
	fawn,
And swing his rump around.

His frisking was at evening
	hours,
For then he lost his fear,
But most before approaching
	showers,
Or when a storm drew near.

Eight years and five rolling
	moons
He thus saw steal away,
Dozing out all his idle noons,
And every night at play.

I kept him for his humour's
	sake,
For he would oft beguile
My heart of thoughts, that
	made it ache,
And force me to a smile.

But now beneath his walnut
	shade
He finds his long last home,
And waits, in snug
	concealment laid,
Till gentler Puss shall come.

He, still more aged, feels the
	shocks,
From which no care can
	save,
And, partner once of Tiney's
	box,
Must soon partake his grave.

**William Cowper
(1731–1800)**

farming community. So prized were stud rabbits that a US breeder is recorded as having paid the enormous sum of £600 for a single Belgian hare buck. The craze lasted for 20 years, and only came to an end when the public learned that the Belgian hare was, in fact, a rabbit, little different to those they could shoot outside their own back door. However, the craze triggered an interest in different breeds of

Two girls play with *their pet rabbits in this early 19th-century Austrian etching.*

rabbit, which led in turn to the foundation of the rabbit fancy (enthusiasts) in the US.

The history of the rabbit in Australia is equally remarkable. Five domestic rabbits were introduced in 1788, but failed to flourish. However, in 1859, a consignment of 24 wild rabbits was imported to a stock farm near Geelong, Victoria. The intention was to raise them for sport. By the 1880s, these rabbits had spread up to 480 km (300 miles) away and, over the next six years, they spread a further 563 (350 miles). The damage rabbits cause to crops is notorious. Their dramatic spread has resulted in endless rabbit fences across Australia, and the intentional introduction of the killer disease myxomatosis in an attempt to control their numbers.

The First World War prompted a large increase in rabbit-keeping in many countries. Food was scarce and rabbits grew quickly on household scraps and food that could not be consumed by other livestock. Large numbers could be kept in a relatively small space, and it was a common sight to see tiers of hutches in the back gardens of many homes.

During the Second World War, UK government records show that there were over 100,000 people claiming bran rations to supplement the diet of their breeding does. The actual number of households keeping rabbits was substantially higher than this; a survey conducted in 1953, when rationing ended, reported that there were three-quarters of a million people breeding rabbits in their back gardens, or on their allotments. Many were members of the 3,000 clubs and societies in existence at the time. This is a sharp contrast to today, when the British Rabbit Council (the official body that controls breed standards and exhibiting in the UK) struggles to keep the number of members above 1,000.

Rabbit fur has long been used in the making of hats, particularly bowlers, and the wool of the Angora can be used to produce very fine knitwear. In 1930, the Fur Board (a co-operative established in the UK to promote the trade) had over 3,000 members, and it was estimated that there were an additional 1,300 people breeding Angoras. Most of this trade was a cottage industry. Imports from abroad, the introduction of myxomatosis in 1953 and the decline in wearing hats put an end to the trade, and the supplementary income it generated for a large number of households.

Pet as fashion accessory: walking the rabbit in Hyde Park, London, in 1939.

At the time the boom in breeding rabbits burgeoned in Victorian Britain, the children of the middle classes were beginning to keep pet rabbits. Among the first was George Stephenson, the inventor of the steam locomotive, who kept rabbits as pets for a great part of his life (1781–1848). Before this, in 1774, the poet, William Cowper (1731–1800), adopted three leverets – Puss, Tiney and Bess – all of which proved to be males. After nursing Puss through a period of ill health, the young hare became tame and spent a considerable time in the garden. The animal used to pull on Cowper's coat to get him to go out into the garden. Bess died young, Tiney lived to be nine years old and Puss even longer, eventually living alongside Marquis, Cowper's spaniel. Tiney's passing prompted Cowper to write his *Epitaph to a Hare* (page 129).

Beatrix Potter, who was later to achieve worldwide fame and a considerable fortune with her tales of Peter Rabbit, Benjamin Bunny and the Flopsy Bunnies, was another early pioneer. From childhood, right through until later life, she kept rabbits both in hutches and inside the house. In *The Tale of Peter Rabbit*, she created what must be a rabbit's dream when she drew Mr McGregor's garden, stocked with row after row of succulent carrots and other vegetables. Although purely fictional, this must be one of the most famous gardens associated with animals. Inspired by Beatrix Potter's illustrations, the British garden designer, Jacquie Gordon, won a gold medal for her recreation of Mr McGregor's garden at the world-famous Chelsea Flower Show in 1999.

EXOTIC BIRDS

When dove-keeping declined, the grander houses took to imported birds in magnificent aviaries. Humphrey Repton designed the aviary at Woburn Abbey for the Fifth Duke of Bedford between 1804 and 1805. The Austrian prince Pückler Muskau visited it in 1826 and wrote that 'the air was literally darkened around us by flights of pigeons, chickens and heaven knows what birds. Out of every bush started gold and silver, pied and common, pheasants; and from the little lake a black swan galloped heavily forward, expressing his strong desire for food in tones like those of a fretful child.'

The aviary at Frogmore was built in 1845 by C.R. Stanley as one of the improvements to the pleasure grounds of Windsor Castle. Elihu Burritt, the American consul in Birmingham, made a visit in 1864 and described it as giving 'the most elegant and comfortable housing to almost every kind of feathered biped known to ornithology.'

One of the best surviving and easily accessible aviaries can be seen at Waddesdon in Buckinghamshire. Baron Ferdinand de Rothschild spared no expense when he built his fine Renaissance house in the last quarter of the 18th century. He levelled the hill where the house and gardens stand, and constructed a little railway to bring the stones as far up the hill as possible; they were hauled the final distance by a special team of Percheron horses imported from Normandy. No expense was spared on the aviary either. It was built in 1889 and is still in use today, unchanged except for the addition of a hospital and kitchens to prepare the food. It houses over 300 birds of 80 different species – including macaws, toucans, glossy starlings and Rothschild grackles.

MAGNIFICENT MENAGERIES

The wealthy and eccentric had both the money and the inclination to indulge their passion for the exotic. Menageries were one way of achieving their desires. Culzean Castle on the west coast of Scotland, for example, has the remains of a monkey house that was built for the Earl of Culzean early in the 19th century. Originally, it looked like a Chinese pagoda, and had a series of roofs that flicked up at the corners.

Birds in the Menagerie at Belvedere Palace, Vienna, taken from an engraving done by Gottleib Theloitt between 1731 and 1740. The palace was built for Prince Eugene following his successful campaigns for the Austrian Emperor against the Turks.

In what is thought to be the first Italianate garden in England, at Wotton House in Surrey, are the remains of a temple for terrapins. Although the gardens have been much altered since they were created by the 17th-century diarist, John Evelyn, the temple is still much as it was when it was built between 1820 and 1830 by either George Evelyn or his son, William John. The latter's animal collection was reputed to include Indian cattle, chameleons, a vulture and kangaroos, which lived loose on Leith Hill until they were exterminated by 'ruthless inidividuals'. The terrapin house has a black-and-white marble floor and a pool fed by a tributary of the River Tillingbourne.

Even as late as 1881, the first Duke of Westminster was transforming Eaton Hall in Cheshire by adding a parrot house, designed by Alfred Waterhouse, to replace a conservatory at the end of the main terrace. The building had its own central heating. The water was heated by a boiler at the rear and ran through brick channels beneath the floor, evaporating through grilles in the floor to create the humidity of a tropical jungle.

By far the most surprising menagerie was that kept by the English poet and artist Dante Gabriel Rossetti in a back garden in Chelsea, London in the late 19th-century. Two armadillos were allowed to run free in the garden. Occasionally they made their way into the next-door garden, where they destroyed choice plants and left large piles of earth. Attempts were made to poison them with a bait of meat laced with prussic acid. The meat disappeared, and so did the armadillos – only to reappear after two months, in a rather dishevelled state having shed their scales. They were eventually rehoused at the Zoological Gardens.

Other oddities in the Rossetti menagerie were a female kangaroo and her son. One morning the Rossettis woke to find the mother dead, after what must have been a fierce family quarrel. The wicked son got his comeuppance a few days later when he was found dead in his cage, having being attacked by the racoon. There was also a wombat, after whose death Rossetti wrote the heartfelt poetic tribute on page 135.

Buffalo, lions and antelope are depicted amongst the statuary of the Menagerie at Belvedere Palace, Vienna in this engraving done by Andr. Friedrich between 1731 and 1740.

THE LAST GOODBYE

Every pet-owner has to prepare themselves to face the eventual death of a beloved pet. Unless they succumb to a serious illness in adult life, or meet with an accident, most of our pets live into old age. For a cat this can mean a lifespan running well into the teens. The natural lifespan of dogs varies by breed, with crossbreeds and smaller breeds tending to live longer than larger breeds. A rabbit that has been fed a healthy diet and is free of dental problems can easily live eight years or more, but again the larger breeds tend to have a shorter life expectancy.

If an animal is obviously suffering in its old age, it is not fair to wait until it dies naturally. Instead, you should consider euthanasia. This is the medical term for 'putting to sleep'. It offers a peaceful, dignified end for a pet that is terminally ill, is experiencing uncontrollable pain, or has lost essential bodily functions and can no longer lead an active life. Your vet will help you to decide when the appropriate time has come, but the final decision must be yours. There may be feelings of guilt, but allowing your pet to leave you painlessly is one of the most important and loving services you can perform for it.

In most cases, the pet's transition into unconsciousness takes place smoothly and quickly, as soon as the overdose of anaesthetic is injected into a vein in one of the forelegs. If the animal is nervous, a sedative may be administered first, but the familiar presence of the owner usually helps to reassure and calm the pet. Some owners cannot bear to watch. This is understandable and, if you cannot, your veterinary practice will respect your decision. However, being present and seeing just how peaceful your pet's final moments were can help you come to terms with your grief much more quickly. The animal falls asleep in seconds, and its breathing and heart stop soon after. There can be no kinder way to end suffering. If you wish, and if you give your veterinary practice prior notice, most will perform euthanasia in your home. For an older pet, this is usually a very comfortable procedure with minimal upset.

Oh how the familiar affections combat
Within this heart, and each hour flings a bomb at
My burning soul! Neither from owl nor from bat
Can peace be gained until I clasp my wombat.

Dante Gabriel Rossetti (1828–82)

Your vet will be able to advise you about disposing of the body and may offer services for cremation and burial. Cats and rabbits can easily be buried in the garden. Place the body in a strong cardboard or wooden box, and cover it with a layer of soil that is at least 60 cm (2 ft) deep. If you want to bury a dog in your garden, you should check with local authorities to ensure that legal and hygiene requirements are observed. Digging a grave large enough and deep enough for anything other than a small dog is a major task. For this reason, it is perhaps advisable to have dogs cremated first and then scatter or bury the ashes in the garden.

A LIVING MEMORIAL

You may want to commemorate the life of your pet. Planting a new shrub or tree is one way of remembering your pet, particularly if you can find a species that reminds you of it. *Exochorda* x *macrantha* 'The Bride', with its abundant show of white flowers in spring, makes a fitting memoiral for a white cat or a West Highland white terrier, while a golden shrub rose would suit a retriever.

No matter whether you had a dog, a cat or a rabbit, and regardless of its breed or colour, there will be a plant that sums up its character and will be a fitting tribute to its companionship. Choose a specimen plant that will be long-lived, and preferably one that brings colour into the garden. Well sited and looked after, it will bring back fond memories for many years.

Planting a living memorial such as a rose or a special shrub is one way of remembering your pet.

STONE MEMORIALS

However, if you want to erect a more permanent memorial, you will be following a well-established tradition. One of the earliest known monuments to a pet dates from 1641, and can be found in the temple of the gardens at Easton Neston in Northamptonshire. Elaborately enscribed on a stone slab that rests on two crudely carved trestles are the words, 'To the memory of PUG'. Jane Austen is thought to have based Mansfield Park on Easton Neston, and 'Pug' could be the model for Lady Bertram's pet dog, 'my poor Pug'.

There are many other tombstones to dogs to be found at great houses throughout Britain. At Dunham Massey in Cheshire, there are a number of 18th-century tombstones to the family's dogs: Cato,

This stone statue
was erected by
parishioners in Fairford,
Gloucestershire, in
memory of the cat
that made Fairford
church its home for
15 years.

Tipler, Old Towzer, Old Virtue, Puce, Bijoux and Lyon. They would have been erected by the First Earl of Warrington, the Second Earl of Warrington, his daughter, Lady Stamford and her son. A portrait of Old Virtue still hangs in the house. Painted by Leonard Knyff in about 1697, it shows a plump brindle pug in front of the house, and a large swooping swallow against a background of deer and sheep. Subsequent generations continued to commemorate their dogs well into the 19th century, with memorials to Gipsy, Beam, Faithful, Dash, Fop and Marquis.

Near this spot
are deposited the Remains of one,
who possessed Beauty without Vanity,
Strength without Insolence,
Courage without Ferocity
and all the virtues of man without his vices.
This praise, which would be unmeaning flattery
inscribed over human Ashes
is but a just tribute to the Memory of
BOATSWAIN, a DOG,
who was born in Newfoundland May 1803
and died at Newstead Nov' 18th 1808

Lord Byron (1788–1824)

Graves at the Presido Pet Cemetery in San Francisco, California.

In the 'Venus Vale' at Rousham in Oxfordshire, William Kent incorporated a memorial stone to Ringwood, a favourite otter hound of General James Dormer. At Wynyard Park in County Durham, there are tombstones and monuments to Lady Londonderry's dogs dating from the first part of the 19th century, with some later additions from the 20th century.

One of the most famous memorials to be found in any garden is that erected by the English poet Lord Byron at Newstead Abbey in Nottinghamshire. It commemorates Boatswain, his Newfoundland, who died of rabies in 1808, and for whom Byron composed a moving epitaph (see page 137). There are three vaults beneath the monument, and in his will of 1811 Byron wrote that he wished to be buried in one, alongside his dog. Such was Byron's commitment to Boatswain that, when the dog was dying, it was reported that 'he, more than once, with his bare hand, wiped the saliva away from the dog's lips during the paroxysms.'

The Duchess of Bedford used the words, 'In life the firmest friend, The first to welcome, foremost to defend' (taken from another of Byron's poems) on the temple she erected at Woburn Abbey in 1916 to mark the death of her Pekinese, Che Foo. The temple, complete with a bronze effigy of the dog, stands by itself in a copse some distance from the house. The Duchess was clearly distraught when the dog died, and wrote in her diary, 'My little Che Foo died. He has been my constant companion for over eleven years and a more faithful and devoted one I shall never have.'

Perhaps because they are more independent, cats do not seem to fare so well: there are few memorials to them. In 1980, the parishioners of Fairford in Gloucestershire erected a memorial to a cat that lived in the church for 15 years, sitting on laps during services. The only notable memorial near an English stately home is in Shugborough, Staffordshire, where a cat sits atop an urn on a huge plinth. It was once believed to be a cat that accompanied Admiral Lord Anson when he sailed around the world between 1740 and 1744. However, the plaque is of a much later date, by which time the Admiral was long dead and the cat would have been 30 or more. A second, and perhaps more likely, theory is that the memorial was erected by the Admiral's brother, Thomas Anson, who inherited Shugborough and transformed the grounds with temples, arches, bridges, ruins and monuments. The cat may have been added at this time. It is known that Thomas Anson liked cats and this memorial may honour one of his pets.

There is no reason why you cannot erect a memorial, or even a monument, to your pet in your own garden. A monumental mason may be happy to make a small headstone or a plaque, using an offcut from a large piece of stone or marble. It could be mounted in a wall and surrounded by a flowering climber or ivy. You could commission a local sculptor to produce something to your own design, but this will undoubtedly be expensive, especially if you have your heart set on a piece that is both lifelike and large. However, placed in the right setting, the statue might become a special feature of the garden, as well as a fitting tribute to a dear departed friend.

This large 19th-century tombstone is dedicated to an obviously much loved Saint Bernard.

Index

PICTURE CREDITS

AKG, London *123*;

Richard Barrett *18, 27, 41, 63, 65, 76, 104, 111, 112l, 112r, 116, 117, 125, 126, 137*;

Jane Burton *12-13, 19, 43*;

Corbis / Austrian Archives *130* / Historical Picture Archives *132-133, 134* / Hulton-Deutsch *131, 139* / Mimmo Jodice *128* / Michael S.Yamashita *138*;

Sylvia Cordaiy Photo Library / Graham Horner *24* / J Howard *55* / Anthony Reynolds *40* / Monika Smith *21, 25*;

Liz Eddison *31, 33, 58b, 60, 94, 95, 107t, 114, 136* / Designer Cherida Seago *35t* / Designer: Alan Sargent *34* / Designer: Jane Sweetser *103* / Designer: Pamela Woods *75*;

Marc Henrie *9, 11, 14, 16, 22, 30, 72, 73, 79, 93*;

Harry Smith Collection *10, 35b, 36-37, 56, 58-59t, 64, 87, 90, 91, 92, 96, 99, 100, 107b*.

ACKNOWLEDGEMENTS

Garden designs by: Clare Palgrave (*Suburban Seclusion*); Jacquie Gordon (*Al-cat-traz* and *The Rural Idyll*)

Garden illustrations by Maggie Read

Rabbit hutch images supplied by: The Hutch Company, Canterbury
Cat and dog flap images supplied by: Staywell, Astra Business Centre, Roman Way, Preston, PR2 5AP

040 L